HARDPRESS.NET
HOME OF HARD-TO-FIND BOOKS

Rejected Articles Parodies, by P.G. Patmore.
by Peter George Patmore

Address:
HardPress
8345 NW 66TH ST #2561
MIAMI FL 33166-2626
USA
Email: info@hardpress.net

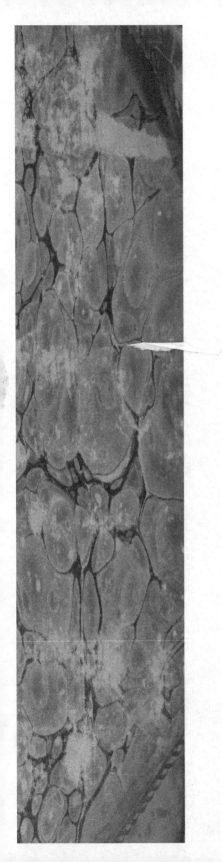

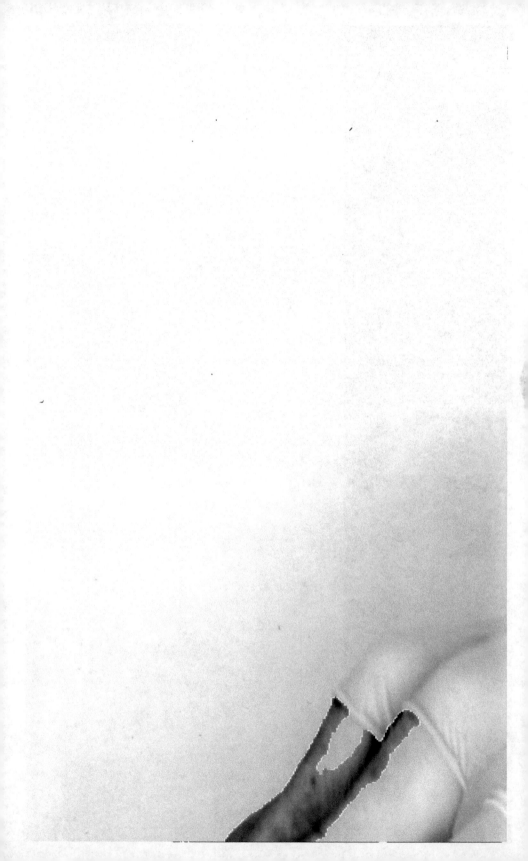

S.H. 1827.

REJECTED ARTICLES.

But be these verities, master Steward?—
—Nay, good Alice, now thou questionest less wisely than is thy wont.
They are that they are; and as that I tell them to thee. If they like thee,
well; if not, it would not make them, though they were ten times verities.

OLD PLAY.

SECOND EDITION.

LONDON:

HENRY COLBURN, NEW BURLINGTON STREET.
1826.

87.

By C. Lamb, W. Corbett, Horace Smith, Leigh Hunt. &c.

LONDON:
IBOTSON AND PALMER, PRINTERS, SAVOY STREET, STRAND.

CONTENTS.

AN UN-SENTIMENTAL JOURNEY.

BY ELIA.

AN UNSENTIMENTAL JOURNEY.

BY ELIA.

READER, thou art haply one of those persons who feel themselves bound in honour to earn (in their own estimation) whatever title it may please others to bestow upon them. If so, reading thyself every day addressed as " reader," (not to reckon the flattering additaments of " gentle," " generous," " tasteful," " learned," " critical," and so forth,) thou hast doubtless felt thyself constrained in conscience to prove the validity of thy title, by perusing every Work (so we puny moderns are minded to denominate our poor, pigmy productions) that comes before thee in a questionable shape : meaning thereby, every one that thou art in the least likely to be questioned about, as to whether it has been perused by thee, or not. In this case, thou hast perchance whiled away an odd half hour now and then, in turning over and tasting the leaves of certain lucubrations, erewhile distilled by driblets from the adust brain of one Elia.

I will suppose thou hast, at any rate. An author would drive a sorry trade indeed, if he were not privileged to *suppose* the case of his having readers. To nine out of ten it is the only means of securing any. And even to the tenth it is much the same.

Thou *hast* read Elia, then, and art therefore not absolutely incognizant of the turn of his humours and oddities, and the character which habit and nature, uniting together, have succeeded (and failed) in impressing upon his mental and bodily man. I put it to thy candour, then, whether, being thus informed, if any but Elia himself were to come and make averment before thee, that they had encountered his pale face, and attenuated form, beyond the confines of his own England, thou wouldest not have treated the tale as an ingenious, albeit an ill-conceived fiction, and greeted the teller with a glance chiefly compounded of the *incredulus odi ?*

Perchance thou sufferest the equivocal happiness of being, like Elia himself, a pun-propounder : (for *punster* is " a weak invention of the enemy " of puns, and not to be uttered by one who honours them :) in which case thou wilt doubtless exclaim, " Elia incontinent ! it cannot be ;" and wilt add,—as Othello

did when a charge of being similarly situated
was made against his gentle mistress,—" I'll not
believe it!"

Thou art altogether in the right, and Elia himself hereby thanks thee for thy well-placed confidence in his consistency. And yet Elia himself is
at the same time constrained to assure thee, that
thou art altogether as wrong as thou art right :
for nothing is more easy (and hard) than to be
entirely both, in regard to one and the same matter.

Look at the transparent tegument (mis-named
paper) on which these uneven words are ecrivated.
On turning it over, thou mayest, by following the
fashion of the Hebrew, read them almost as well
on the wrong side as on that which is not the
right.   Glance thine eye, too, towards the top of
the page. It is dated " Calais."   There is no
gainsaying the fact.   Elia is, like Bottom, " translated " from his own modest, low-roofed parlour,
looking out upon the little Ever-Green (here they
would think it a strip of baize) that stretches
before the plain, uni-painted door of his quiet
domicile, in the suburban village of " Shacklewell,
near Hackney, near London, England—" for such
is the endless supererogation which he is obliged
to inscribe upon the letter which he has just dis-
patched (what a word, when they tell me it will

not reach her these three days!) to his dear cousin Bridget—he is translated, I say, from the above spot (apt title, *spot*, when compared with the " infinite space " of which at present he is denizen) to a magnificent Scene in the Play which seems to be continually acting here, called " Dessin's Hotel."

Reader, if thou wilt accord me a more than ordinary share of thy patience, I will recount how this seeming inconsequentiality came about : for thy confidence in its unlikelihood merits *my* confidence in return.

As I have begun *supposing* for thee, I may as well go on. I suppose, then, that thou art not ignorant of the signal change which, a brief while ago, (brief it is by the book, though to me it already seems an age—so crowded has it been with thoughts, feelings, fancies, imaginations, and what not), took place in my terrene condition, in virtue of my becoming a " superannuated man." Some of the consequences of this change I have elsewhere related ; but the " greatest is behind."

If thou hast perused, reader, the relation I have just alluded to, touching the first impressions of a man who just begins to feel his freedom press upon him, with a weight

   " Heavy as frost, and deep almost as life,"

thou wilt readily conceive * * * *. In short, something was evidently * * * *. Besides which * * * *.

And moreover, what so natural to expect from Elia, under extraordinary circumstances, as that which nobody who knew him *would* expect from him?

Suffice it that I " made up my mind" to go. (The phrase is singularly "*german* to the matter"— that is to say, not within some hundreds of miles of expressing what it is meant to express : but let it pass.) So I clapped a shirt in my pocket; (it is hard that we cannot do the simplest of actions without incurring the suspicion of being *imitatores servum pecus:* people will say I borrowed the idea, of putting a clean shirt in my pocket, from Yorick : as if the abstract idea of a clean shirt did not instinctively become a part of every man's conscious-ness, the moment he thinks of leaving home !) I put a shirt into my pocket; hurried a kiss, with no very firm or florid lip, on the faded cheek of my cousin Bridget ; (we have never been separated for twelve hours since we came together twice twelve years agone); got into the Shacklewell stage, as was my wont every morning for all those years ; and as wont also, when it set me down at the Bank as usual, I proceeded towards my accustomed haunt

in Leadenhall Street, and should assuredly have
taken my accustomed seat on the accustomed
stool, but that, just as I was stepping up, under the magnificent portico of that Palace of
Commerce, I felt an *unaccustomed* weight—*not*
upon my heart, reader : I declare to thee that *that*
waxed lighter and lighter every step I approached
towards the spot where its rest had so long been
set up ; but—bobbing against the calf of my sinister leg. It was the bundle that Bridget had
squeezed into my pocket. This roused me from
my reverie ; and I turned back, just so as to reach
in time the great monster that was to bear me on
its back, (not more against *my* will than that of the
water,) to the shores of France.

THE VOYAGE.

I hate all Steam, and all that it can do ; except
when it comes singing its soft sweet tune, from
out the mouth of a half bright, half black tea-
kettle, on a December evening fire. But above
all I hate it, when, as I have chanced to see it
once or twice, it gets possession (like a bad demon)
of some otherwise dead hull, and drives it, scram-
bling, splashing, heaving, straining, and roaring
along, *up* our noble river Thamisis, belching forth

fire and smoke, and invading, terrifying, and polluting the sweet solitudes of Twickenham and Richmond, with its hideous brawl.

I once watched one of these new " infernal machines," as it came towards me while I was wandering under those fine old trees near Brandenburg House; and I perceived that the poor victim of Steam was straining itself against the water, and lifting its breast partly out, at every stroke of its relentless task-master; just as a half-heart-broken stage-coach horse strains against the collar, up a steep hill, at the stroke of the whip. And yet the stroke came (as it does in the other case) as regular as clock-work. There was " damnable iteration " in it; it sent me home sick; and I have hated Steam better than ever, ever since.

And yet here did I find myself, at eleven of the clock on a sweet sunshiny day of September, in the actual clutches of this abhorred power; prepared, nay *expecting* to be borne by it—to the clouds, as likely as not, in a clap of thunder; and to come down from thence, scorched to a cinder, and hiss as I fell into the water, and sunk at once to the bottom like a bit of burnt coal!

When I am in good health, (good, I mean, for me,) and have my wits about me, I feel but one care concerning Death: it is that I may meet him not absolutely unlooked for, and in my own bed with the old dark crimson damask hangings; and with my cousin Bridget *not* beside me.   And yet here was I, willingly, or rather wilfully, putting myself in the way of half a dozen of the most hideous of all deaths, (for the name of Steam is not one but Legion,) without even having a choice in them.

It was not to be thought of.   So I seated myself at once on the first projection that came to hand—looked down towards my feet—and as I heard the bowels of the great creature begin to grumble within it, and felt its body move beneath me, luckily the thought came across me of Sinbad the sailor, when he was inveigled, by some unaccountable fascination, to trust himself on the back of the Old Man of the Sea.

This recollection, by virtue of the associations I had connected with it, partly restored me from myself; and I did not return till I was called back by an indescribable jargon of tongues, as if some foreign Bedlam or Bank Rotunda had broke loose at midnight—from which I could gather nothing, but that I was actually arrived in the port of Calais.   But this was more than enough; so I resigned myself into the hands of fate, under the form of a French waiter, and after a few ceremonies which I did not seek to understand, found myself in a spacious sleeping apartment of

DESSIN'S HOTEL.

I am not the person to go gadding after other men's fancies. I have enough to do to keep pace with my own. I was never fond of " follow my leader," even at school. I would not follow, and did not want to lead. And yet, reader, I am fain to confess to thee, that peradventure if it had not been for Hogarth and Sterne, " The gates of Calais" would never have shut upon Elia ; and even if they had, the hundred harpies from its Hotels would in all probability have divided him amongst them, instead of one being permitted to spirit him away in the name of " Dessin" in particular.

To be sure there is, in regard to the latter point, something to be said for the determination which the before-named *one* had evidently formed, as to the necessity of my following *him*, and no one else. " Sare—you *shall* go to Mister Dessin," he repeated, close into my ear, twenty times at least. And when a man *shall* do a thing, he must. So I went.

I need scarcely tell the " travelled " reader, that on this first moment of my setting foot in a foreign land, I was in no disposition to note very carefully the localities through which I was led by the absolute person into whose hands I fell. It must suffice to say, that I retired to my unrest, in the midst of indistinct and confused visions, of an immeasurable Gateway, an illimitable Court-yard, an incomprehensible Coach and Horses, an unintelligible Chambermaid, and an inaccessible Bed.

My dreams on that night favoured me by being more fantastical than I have known them for many a long year : for, as I think I have otherwhere informed thee, reader, I am but a poor hand at dreaming. My dreams put me out of conceit of myself. *Anybody* might dream them. But on that night, methought, among other matters, that I suddenly sank into the sea, and was (Jonas-like) swallowed by a whale ; and that the passage through his throat to his belly, where I lodged, was exactly like that between Lombard Street and Cornhill, where Mr. Myers the fishmonger lives, and that it smelt of fish much the same as that does ; and that, when I had got through it, I found myself in a great paved court-yard, the extremities of which I could not see, which was partly lighted by what seemed to be the creature's great lidless eye; and that, while I was passing across its dreary spaciousness, I heard a number of what the children call *crackers* go off just outside, and then saw, by the glimmering light, a sort of carriage like Neptune's conch come clattering in, drawn by three animals, (a-breast,) which seemed to be compounded of half Meux's dray-horses, half mermaids; and from the side of one of which I could see depending that enormous *sign* of a Boot and Spur, which has so long delighted the eyes of all the urchins who inhabit the Borough of Southwark. Methought, too, as I looked up towards the ceiling of my new apartment, it seemed to be intersected by enormous black beams, just like my cousin's great barn at Mackery End, in Hertfordshire, where I used to sit upon the wheat-sheaves, and read Burton: and yet I could see the stars shine through it.

Then all of a sudden I heard an enormous explosion, and found myself flying through the air, seated astride upon a great piece of burning wood, rudely carved into the form of a rocking-horse; which I held by, exactly as John Gilpin in the prints does by the neck of *his* horse. And I remember very well fancying, as I shot through the air, and got glimpses of the flaming tail of my steed flaring out behind me, how the philosophers of London would proclaim me a Comet, and call it by the name of Elia !

Then, as suddenly, I found myself quietly seated in a great unknown room, by the side of an unknown tent-like erection, beneath which was what bore some resemblance to a bed; and around were various objects, which I did not take the trouble to examine—especially as, in divesting myself of my nether garments, preparatory to trying whether the seeming bed *was* a bed or not, I found that they came away piecemeal, and were in fact scorched to a cinder.

This seemed to disconcert me more than the nature of the accident warranted; and I got up hastily, to ring the bell, and call for another pair, just as I would have called for a pint of wine—(for I now seemed to recollect that I was at an inn) —when, taking hold of the great ring which hung to the bell-rope, I pulled it somewhat impatiently —and lo! it seemed to produce as miraculous effects as the pull or cut of the Sultan, in the Arabian Nights, at the ring revealed to him by his faithful Vizier. Mr. Dessin's hotel seemed to stand before me for a moment, like a scene on the stage, and then, like that, sunk into the earth at the sound of the bell I had pulled——the Gates of Calais (which formed part of the *back* scene) came clattering about the ears of their astonished keepers——the Sea in the distance was changed into the Strand, with its gas-lights and coaches just when the Play is over;——and the next moment I found myself seated beside my cousin Bridget, in our own quiet parlour, and Betty was just entering to ask whether it was the bed-candle that I had rung for.

My late friend Tobin makes Juliana say, (prettily enough, under the circumstances of the scene, I remember,) "we cannot help our dreams." But what is a great deal worse, we cannot help *telling* them. If all the above incoherencies had actually and *bona fide* befallen me, I verily believe, reader, I should have had too much respect for thy time and patience (to say nothing of my taste) to think of relating them to thee; because there is nothing to be extracted from them in any way tending to thy moral instruction, or even to thy mental delectation. But because they have *not* happened to me, and could not, I have been tempted to record them.

This is one of the most unpardonable impertinencies of which any of us are guilty. If I ever for a moment think that my cousin Bridget talks too much, or not wisely, it is when she

is telling me of some strange dream that she
has had.   Nobody should ever tell their dreams,
but C———.   Even de Q—— should leave it off,
now that he has left off that which made his
dreams so marketable a commodity.

Travelled reader, I would fain have thee believe,
that in the midst of my humours and oddities, I
am not an altogether unreasonable specimen of
the human animal—I mean in respect of those of
his intellectuals by which he carries on the daily
business of his life.   Thou opinest, perhaps, that
because I have hitherto been content (howbeit,
" on compulsion," yet not the less sincerely therefore) to pass my days within the atmosphere of
the Great City, (for my retreat at Shacklewell is a
retreat from her noise only, not a recession from
beneath that noble canopy of congregated clouds
which constantly hangs over her head, queen-like,)
—therefore I do keck and reluct at the taste and
odour of any atmosphere which has the demerit of
being more pure, and quarrel with every form
that comes before me, not moulded on the accustomed model.

In this thou deceivest thyself, and discreditest
me.   In respect of feelings, fancies, modes of
belief, and the like, I do agnize a certain degree of wilful predisposition.   But in what re-

lates to form, to matter, to manner, to taste, to sound, to smell, in short all pertaining to our sensuous and animal nature, I do strenuously assert my entire freedom from prejudice and pre-occupation. What if I do cherish a somewhat inordinate passion for Roast Pig, and am even prepared (peace-lover as I am) to place spear in rest to prove the pre-eminence of that dulcet refection, over every other in the whole circle of my *mundus edibilis?* Yet assuredly I speak but of *my* world. I am no mad-brained Quixote in this matter. Far be it from me to believe, *prima facie*, much less to insist, that a sucking Kangaroo, treated in a similar manner, may not be as good. (Perhaps my friend B. F. is able to speak to this point.) And if your Cannibal, who is " your only emperor for diet," were to twit me with the superlative savoriness of a roasted Christian, assuredly I should not dispute the point with him. I am not in a condition to determine. I have never tasted one; and according to the calculable probabilities of the case, never may.

After this open confession, reader, thou wilt not see cause to admire overmuch, when I assure thee, that my morning ablutions were no less refreshing than usual, albeit they were performed from a

c

pie-dish in place of that hemispherical receptacle
which *we* employ for that purpose ; that my tea
tasted not the less fragrant for being sipped from
a cup that a bee might have mistaken for a tulip ;
and that I did not *fancy* myself in worse than my
ordinary health when I *felt* myself in better,
merely because my braekfast was brought to me
in my bed-room.

In truth, whether that the sea air of yesterday
has braced up the bands of my spirits, or that
the entire novelty of the scene which I find before
my eyes on waking this morning has loosened
and set them vibrating, (for I give thee thy
choice, reader, between the material and the
moral theory), certain it is, that they are in better
than their usual trim.   And as I have often given
thee the proceeds of their peevishness and want
of self-controul, it is but fair that thou shouldst
have thy share in their more " blest condition."

But look not for any regular narrative from me.
A *series* of events, even when, as my friend W.
hath it, they are " linked each to each by natural
piety," is what I am altogether incapable of following, even in idea.   My intellectuals have, at
some period or other of their existence—whether
before they appertained to me, the man Elia, or

since, I guess not—undergone a sort of disjoint-
ment or dislocation, which has shut up some of
those alleys or avenues by which the several apart-
ments communicated with each other and formed
a suite. And the consequence is, that though
each room may be as well adapted to its appointed use as another's, and may be as fitly furnished, (though I say not that they be so), yet
many of them can only be come at by out-of-the-
way means—such as climbing in at the window, or
dropping down the chimney.

Touching the sky of France, and the atmosphere that fills its blue breadth, I like them well,
as a change. They seem to breathe into me a
buoyancy, (why not write it *boy*ancy?) that I
have not lately felt, (I confess it), even in the
greenest of the green places that neighbour my
suburban home; or in the pleasant fields of Hertfordshire, or of more distant Devon. It is as if
they were impregned with a vinous spirit, drawn
forth by the glances of that " hot amorist," the
Sun, from the innumerous vine-clad vallies on
which he looks in his lightsome course. In England
the open air, when it *is* open, never fails to still
that restless stir " which hangs upon the beatings
of the heart." It hushes it, as a nursing-mother

hushes her infant, "while pap-content is making."
(I speak of it at its best.)   We can fall asleep
in its arms ; or fancy that we are sleeping—which
is better.   It is lulling sweet, and soft ; balmy, as
if distilled from the breath of flowers.   It is
dream-compelling—the mother of sweet meditations.   When all wrapt about by it like a soft
garment, we feel that

"If it were now to die, 't were now to be most happy :"

so full and sure is the bliss—so quiet, yet so consummate.   But *here*—hey for old Ben's "New
Inn, or the light of heart !"   No dreaming here
—no meditations—no mild melancholy—no pleasant despondencies.   And as for dying, it is a
thing clean out of the question.   It cannot be.
Death himself seems dead and gone.   He could
not live upon such life-creating food.   He is
fairly starved out.   Or if he comes at all, it
must be "like a thief in the night."   There can
be no such thing as dying in the day-time, here.

I never could make out what it was which
created that anomaly in morals and manners, the
French character.   But I have tasted their air,
and my difficulties have melted away into it.
I am a Frenchman myself!   I go about on the

tips of my toes; and move my arms from my
sides " with an air;" and hum snatches of old
French tunes; and step aside when I meet the
blooming peasant women in the market-place,—
gracefully bowing the head of my imagination as
they pass, and scattering flowers (of fancy) in
their path. I must return incontinently; or there
will be two Elias—which were too many; and
yet not one—which were too few.

Let me, however, set down a few notes, as me-
morials of the danger I have run, of losing my
identity, and becoming " sophisticated." And
first, let me do justice to M. Dessin's Hotel. It is
an Inn for the Titans to have stopped at. Its court-
yard is like one of the great Quadrangles at Oxford,
in all but the stillness and the green. It is, to
other inns, what the India-house is to other count-
ing-houses. It seems built in mockery of us
puny moderns; and it were idle to inquire if it is
ever full,—for if every room were occupied it
would still be empty.—Sallying forth from its
great gateway into the street, (of which a tenth part
of the Hotel forms half,) you feel " cabinned,
cribbed, confined,"—as when passing out of Lin-
coln's-inn-fields into Turnstile. If M. Dessin
could be prevailed on to build a Church in the
centre of the court-yard, and turn one of the

rooms into a Theatre, it would be a complete thing.

THE MARKET-PLACE.

It is Saturday, and Market-day ; and if, reader, thou art not susceptible of Market-day in a great country-town, thou art not for Elia's money ; or rather he is not for thine. It is among the prettiest sights in nature : in the nature of art, I mean. Such nut-brown faces, with the red bloom breaking through them ! Such teeth, shining forth through such lips ! Such clean clothes, and such fly caps ! I have not, like de Q——, been a great frequenter of markets—especially London ones, at night. But of all the markets that I *have* seen, commend me to this one of Calais. If all England can shew a dozen such sights, once a week throughout the year, it is a better place than I think it—which is much. And if every great town in France can shew such a one, it is a better place than *anybody* thinks it—which is much more.

In passing from the Port last night, in custody of the commissioner (so the little ragged rogue calls himself) whose will, or rather whose *shall* it was that I should go to Mister Dessin's hotel in particular, I observed that we traversed a great open Square, shut in by high houses on every side, and empty of every living and dead thing—except the moon-light—which is neither. To-day that Square is one unbroken mass of moving life and beauty, and of that without which they are not worth having. I never saw anything so brilliant ;—not even the Dutch pictures of similar scenes. Indeed, I never greatly affected *pictures* of this kind of scene. In a picture they can neither be *idealized* nor *realized :* and the merit of pictures consists in their doing either one or other of these, in regard to the scene or object they profess to represent. The old Italians often did the first, and the old Flemings the second ; and the moderns do neither. But this Market is a better thing, in its way, than any of them ever did. Come with me into it, reader, and let us see of what it consists.

On first entering it, from the street where I sojourn, (yclept " Royal," on account, I suppose, of its containing the Prince of Hotels), it looks, to a general glance over it, something like what the great Tulip bed, in Mr. Smith's Nursery at Dalston, must appear to the " microscopic eye" of a fly—so intermingled are the colours of the such an air of happy independence, overflowing every now and then into sparkling streams of mirth ;—all this, I freely confess to thee, reader, I never witnessed before. I do not know how it may be with thee ; but for me, it has filled me with a serious joy, interfused with a still more serious melancholy and misgiving, which I do not very well know how to entertain. *We*, in England, cannot shew such a sight as this for our lives. And if a state like this of France *can* shew it, at a stone's throw from our shores, and after all that she has suffered and performed, there must be "something rotten" in—but hold, hold, my gentle friend, Elia ! if thou lovest me (or thyself) hold ! Let thy wild fancy intermeddle as it will with all things else ; but let it leave Politics to patriots, parrots, and popular preachers. Shun it as thou wouldst a pestilence. Knowest thou not the wreck and ruin it has wrought among thy dearest friends ? Has it not made * * * * * but let us have done with it.

These beautiful realities, from which we for a moment turned away so idly, are butter-women. Each is standing (not sitting) behind a milk-white wooden receptacle, over which she bends grace-fully, with a hand on each knee, and the cover of which she lifts up on the approach of a customer, and discloses her little store. It may be worth, perhaps, altogether—including the basket of eggs which always accompanies it—as much as we (erewhile) clerks used to give for our daily mutton chop and pint of wine, at a paltry tavern in the city. And yet she who owns it reckons the mere profit on it—which she has already realized in imagination—a little possession. And that she gets more than " a living" upon the interchange of it, is evident from the tasty trimness of her attire, its delicate cleanness and propriety, and above all from those great yellow gold ear-ornaments ("tops and drops," I remember we used to call them, when they were in vogue among us) that hang down from her ears to her very shoulders, where they rest. Her attire is fashioned as follows : and it differs from all her tribe only in the relative arrangement of its colours. On the body a crimson jacket, of a thick, solid texture, and tight to the shape ; but without any pretence at ornament. This is met at the waist (which is neither long, nor short, but exactly where nature placed it) by a dark blue petticoat, of a still thicker texture, so that it hangs in large plaits where it is gathered in behind. Over this, in front, is tied tightly round the waist, so as to keep all trim and compact, a dark apron, the

string of which passes over the little fulled skirt
of the jacket behind, and makes it stick out
smartly and tastily, while it clips the waist in.
The head-gear consists of a sort of mob cap,
nothing of which but the edge round the face can
be seen, on account of the kerchief (of flowered
cotton) which is passed over it, hood fashion, and
half tied under the chin.   This head-kerchief is
in place of the bonnet—a thing not to be seen
among the whole five hundred females who make
up this pleasant show.   Indeed, varying the
colours of the different articles, this description
applies to every dress of the whole assembly ; except that in some the fineness of the day has dispensed with the kerchief, and left the snow-white
cap exposed ; and in others, the whole figure (except the head) is coyishly covered and concealed
by a large hooded cloak of black cloth, daintily
lined with silk, and confined close up to the
throat by an embossed silver clasp, but hanging
loosely down to the heels, in thick, full folds.
The petticoat is very short ; the trim ancles are
cased in close-fit hose of dark, sober, slate colour ;
and the shoes, though thick and serviceable like
all the rest of the costume, fit the foot as neatly
as those which are not made to walk in.

I declare these picturesque people (the epithet

belongs to them more than to any I ever saw, for
they look as if they had just walked out of pictures) have made quite a delineator of me.   I
never was so descriptive before.   How sayest
thou, reader?   This is the age of authors who
write with the pencil instead of the pen.   Shall I
enlist myself among the number, and issue proposals for publishing by subscription a set (of all
things in the world) of "French Scenes and Cos-
tumes?"   I, who do not pretend even to see,
much less to make others see, any thing more
of human life, and its results, than those little
obliquities and excrescencies which start out from
the strait line and dead level of it, and are over-
looked by its other spectators?   To me, those per-
-sons and things which are like other persons and
things, are like nothing—or they *are* nothing, for
I do not observe them long enough to see them.
They slip off my sensorium without making any
impression upon it.

No; I may, perhaps have given, above, an intelligible account of a common thing; because to
me it was not common, and because, moreover, there
is something in it which, if I mistake not, is es-
sentially characteristic and peculiar.   But I must
stop in time, or I shall put in jeopardy any little
credit I may have gained for seeing what others

do not, by putting down as strange and worthy of record what every body else regards in the light of a level common-place. . I will therefore leave thee, reader, (and thou canst scarcely be on a spot better adapted to provide thee with a few hours, of innocent delectation), in the midst of the grand Place of Calais, on the Market-day of the first Saturday in September, eighteen hundred and twenty-five ;—assuring thee, in all sincerity, that if thou lookest about thee with an observant eye, and a mind made soft by sympathy with the crowd of happy humans that surround thee, thou shalt carry away a throng of impressions that will stand thee in better stead, in thy passage through this valley of (*not* " the shadow of death," but) the sunshine of life, than will, though he should write till doomsday, all the crude thoughts, and dreamy fancies, and wild imaginations, and super-subtle distinctions—all the false truths, and the true falsehoods of thy sincere well-wisher,

ELIA.

RICH AND POOR.

A LETTER FROM WILLIAM COBBETT TO THE PLOUGHBOYS AND
LABOURERS OF HAMPSHIRE.

RICH AND POOR.

A LETTER FROM WILLIAM COBBETT TO THE PLOUGHBOYS AND LABOURERS OF HAMPSHIRE.

MY HONEST FRIENDS AND FELLOW COUNTRYMEN,

1. I HAPPENED to be down in your parts the other day, about a little Turnpike business— (perhaps you've heard of the pretty game I've been playing up lately, among the rascally Jews who have got all the London Turnpike Trusts into their hands, and are filling their own pockets by picking those of other people)—I say, happening to be down in the neighbourhood of Botley, I took a little pains to find out whether you are as well off now as when I was living among you; and I was sorry to hear sad complaints about you from some of my old farming friends.

2. Times are a little changed with the landlords and the farmers since then, to be sure—

D

thanks to the Paper Money and the Corn Bill ;
as I told them over and over again it would be.
And when times change for the worse with *them*,
they are not very likely to change for the better
with *you*.   When the head and body are cold,
the hands and feet are seldom very warm.   It is
as I said it would be, years ago.   There is'nt
work for half of you ; and those that there is
work for don't get half paid ; and the old ones
among you are obliged to take up with the work-
house ; and the young ones to break stones to
mend the roads, that the rich parsons and parliament-men may roll along smoothly, as they
loll their lazy carcases back in their fine carriages
—one of which, by the bye, and the cost of its
keep, would provide twenty of you and your
families with wholesome food, warm clothing,
and a nice little snug cottage over your heads,
for twenty years to come !

3. I hear too that some of you have actually
the audacity (so the said parsons and parliament-men think and call it) not to be content
with this amusing occupation of everlasting
stone cracking ; or even to be quite satisfied
with holding the plough from morning till night
for ten pence a-day ; and have been trying to
better yourselves by making your way up to

town *to get places.* Now *this* information, my good lads, is what has tempted me to put aside many other important matters that I had in hand, and address you the present letter.

4. And so, because matters are going a little hard with you, and your accustomed labour will not procure all that you would like to have, (and that, I admit, you *ought* to have,) you are getting tired of your present condition, and hankering after others that you ought to be proud of knowing nothing about. Because ploughboys and labourers don't get quite so much as they used to do, and as you hear is to be got by other occupations, you begin to think that ploughing and labouring are not the best kinds of work for those whose lot it is to work for their bread.

5. But I should be glad to know how you can change your condition for a better. What occupation is more honourable than husbandry? What is more manly, more healthful, more pleasant ? I tell you what, my lads, I shrewdly suspect that some of your rantipole Squires have been filling their houses with visiters from London for the sporting season, who have brought down with them a pack of grooms, valets, lacqueys, and other lazy hounds, and that these chaps have got among you at the Alehouse, while their masters

D 2

were getting drunk together at the Hall, and have
instilled some of their cursed notions into your
heads, about the pleasures of a London life, and
the delights of having large wages and little work,
and of being dizened out in flashy clothes, and
riding behind their masters, or perhaps sitting
cheek-by-jowl beside them, in some gimcrack
gingerbread gig, so that nobody but themselves
can tell which is which!

6. But do you pretend to have English blood
in your veins, and yet tell me that *this* is a life
fit for an Englishman? Would you, who rise
with the sun, and sally out into the sweet morning air, and having driven your team a-field,
seize the smooth-rubbed handle of your glittering plough, and whistle at your work till breakfast time, while the blackbird is whistling back
to you from the copse, the lark singing merrily
in the sunshine above your head, and the wholesome steam of the new-turned earth is rising
all about you, and mixing with the sweet breath
of the hawthorn; would *you*, I say, who can
live such a life as this, and *have* lived it, change
it to be groom of the stable and hold the stirrup
to some lubberly lord, who is himself perhaps
groom of the bedchamber and holds (I won't say
what) to a king, who is himself lacquey to all of

us, for he receives our pay and wears our livery? Would *you*, who when your day's work is over, are as much your own masters as any lord in the land; and more; and are at no man's beck and call; (as no one who bears the name of *man* ought to be;) would *you* change your condition, to become the servant of a servant's servant, and not be able to call your soul your own; merely because you can get a few shillings in a year more wages by it? Would *you*, I say, do this? Then shame and short commons be your portion!

7. But no; you would not do it. I know you would not. I have not lived in the midst of you all these years, and spent the greater part of them in trying to cultivate a spirit of independence among you, and all for nothing. You would not, I'm sure you would not, be content to be slaves to the rich, merely because you happen to be what they (the rich) call poor.

8. But, my good lads, I'm almost afraid you don't properly understand the meaning of those words " Rich " and " Poor." And if you don't I'll be sworn the parson of the parish won't teach you. So I will. You must know, then, that the London Press—you've heard of the Press, I suppose; the base, beggarly, lying Press; the cowardly, skulking, scoundrel Press; the Newspaper

Press; you've heard of this *thing*, by means of which half a score cunning knaves contrive to gull, hoodwink, and bamboozle half the nation, (and would do the whole if it was not for me,) and cram their pockets with pelf at the same time. I wish I had time to put you up to a few of their tricks. But I'll just give you a notion how some of them are *paid* for what they do; and then you may give a pretty good guess as to *what* it is that they do, to get paid after that fashion. It was but the other day that a fellow named Clement; a great fat bull-necked pot-bellied chap he is now ; but I knew him when he was so thin and half starved that he could have crept in and out at a rat-hole. Well; this fellow set up a thing called a "Sunday Paper;" in which he used to collect together all the lies that had been hatched in the course of the week, and add a lot more of his own invention, and then persuade the people, by his puffing advertisements, to buy all this trash, and read it to one another of a Sunday, and fancy that they were as much concerned in it as if it had all been gospel.

9. Well; this fellow, I say, after having carried on a roaring trade in these lies for some time, found the money tell in at such a rate, that he bethought himself, if he could but contrive to

bring his pigs to market seven times a week instead
of once, his profits would be seven times as
much as they were before: for he's one of those
people who have just sense enough to know that
seven is seven times as much as one. Accordingly,
the other day (that is a few months ago) another
newspaper chap of the name of Perry; a paltry,
pitiful fellow, who used to kick his heels in the
antichambers of lords and dukes, and was sometimes allowed to lick his fingers at the lower end
of their dinner tables, on condition of puffing their
parliament speeches next day; this last chap,
I say, happened to die just pat, as if on purpose, for the other (Clement) to pop into his
place.

10. But how was he to do this? for places
that are worth having are not to be got by asking for. *How* was he to get into this place?
Why by *cash* to be sure. He determined to
buy it. *Buy* a newspaper! A thing, the success
of which (putting merit and demerit out of the
question) depends entirely on the person who
conducts it! and the person who had hitherto
conducted this was dead! But no matter:
Clement determined to *buy* this place, left vacant by the death of Perry. (And what place,
by the bye, is *not* to be bought in London, if you

know how to set about making the bargain?)
In short, Clement bought this defunct daily paper,
called the Morning Chronicle; for defunct it must
be when Perry was so; since the Morning Chronicle meant neither more nor less than a sheet of
paper, on which he (Perry) chose to print anything that *he* had to say on any topic that might
be the talk of the hour. Clement *bought* it, however. And how much do you think he *gave* for
it? for *this* is the point to which I wish to direct
your attention. How much do you think he *paid*
for it?

11. Why " fools and their money are soon
parted; perhaps a matter of a hundred pounds;"
I hear some of you say. A hundred pounds!
What do you say to FORTY THOUSAND? FORTY
THOUSAND POUNDS!!!—This is what Clement
paid, for the privilege of venting his lies six times
a-week oftener than he had hitherto done, under
the name of the Morning Chronicle. FORTY
THOUSAND POUNDS!!! Enough to keep you
and all your families from want, all through the
county, if you were never to do another day's
work while you live! What do you say to this,
my honest friends?—You see *lying* is the trade
to get rich by, after all. It is better than farming, even when wheat is 90s. a quarter.

12. But I must get back to the subject on which I began to address you. I was saying that I'm afraid you do not exactly see the true difference between what are called the Rich and the Poor. And I don't know how you should, when it has been, any time these thirty years, the sole business of this base Press to throw dust into your eyes to prevent you from seeing the truth, and dirt at all those who, like me, are able and willing to shew it you?

13. Ask, for instance, the Times newspaper; the hireling, hellish Times; the bloody Old Times; who calls *me* " old Cobbett:" the brute beast! as if I was'nt young enough to be pretty sure of living to see him and all his base crew carted, and to spit upon their graves! Ask, I say, this infamous " Times " newspaper what's the difference between a " rich " man and a " poor " one, and the advantages or disadvantages of each; and it's ten to one but he tells you that the chief difference consists in the one being able, and the other not able, to buy *his* paper!

14. But the dolt forgets (or at least he would have *you* forget; for I'll take good care *he* shall never forget it) that there is such a writer as William Cobbett in the world; who glories, and ever will, in telling the truth to those who cannot

afford to purchase it, even if there were any one
else to offer it them ; and who thus puts an end
to the distinction between " poor " and " rich,"
and places them both on a level in point of intellect and knowledge ; which is the only real
riches.   The pay that pleases *me* is the good I'm
doing.   I don't deny that I like money well
enough ; especially when it comes out of the
pockets of those who have plundered it from
the people ; for I know what to do with it better
than they do : and what is more, I *deserve* it ;
which nobody will say of *them*.   But of the
poor I scorn to take a penny beyond what is just
enough to pay me for the paper and print of what
I write for them.   As for the writing itself, they
are welcome to that.   My Register is a nice little
book containing *thirty-two* pages ; not a great,
flapping, fly away thing, containing only *four*
pages ; like the offspring of the vagabond Press.
And yet the price of *my* THIRTY-TWO pages is
sixpence, and the price of *their* FOUR pages is
sevenpence ! !

15. Now mark me, my friends.   All that I
desire is, that in London (the *Metropolis*, as it
is nicknamed by scholars ; the great WEN, as *I*
call it, who, thank God ! am no scholar) all I
wish by way of remuneration for *my* labours is,

that all the mechanics and artizans in this wen would form themselves into little clubs or companies, of either six or twelve, as their circumstances will permit, and each lay down his penny or halfpenny (as the case may be) to buy my Register, and read it in turn, or to one another; —that in every market town throughout the kingdom of England, Scotland, and Ireland similar clubs be formed, and also that every tap-room be compelled (by its customers I mean) to take one copy, in order to have it at hand to refer to in case of need;—and lastly, that every village and hamlet in the United Kingdom be supplied with one or more copies, according to its size; the said copies to be paid for in any manner most convenient to the persons interested. The trifling profit that would be derived from this, is all I desire. As for the parlour people; the parsons, the squires, and all *their* gang; they may read the Register, or not, just as they please.

16. But to the point, as to who is " Rich," and who " Poor," in the real practical meaning of these words. My Lord Lackwit, who lives at the great " Place," as they call it; (I need not point him out more particularly, for you know who I mean, well enough); this " Lord" has an income of forty thousand pounds a year; or three

thousand three hundred and thirty-three pounds
a month ; or eight hundred pounds a week ; or
a hundred and ten pounds a day !! This is, in
round numbers, the amount of his income ; of the
money that he has to spend every day in his life
throughout the year. There are several of these
" Lords," elsewhere, who have twice or three times
as much as this. But we will take him as an
example, because you *know* something of him, and
will therefore know whether what I shall have to
say about him is true or not.

17. This " Lord," then, has a sum of money
coming to him every *day* of his life, which amounts
to as much as would keep *four* of your families in
comfort for *a whole year.* Now, is this " Lord " a
" Rich" man, or a " Poor" one ? You laugh at
the question ; and so would he if it were put to
him. But if it were *I* who put it, and he had
sense enough to understand and feel the reply
which I should make to it, he would pretty soon
begin to laugh on the wrong side of his mouth.
But is he a " rich" man ? I mean rich in point
of mere money ; for the riches of comfort and
content are not what we are now talking about.
We shall come to that afterwards. Is this Lord
" rich" in point of money ?

18. Let us see. But, in order that we may

understand each other clearly, let us start on this principle, that a man is " rich" or " poor," in proportion as he has *much* left, or *less than nothing*, after providing himself and his family with the necessaries of life.

19. In the first place this " Lord" has to provide food, lodging, and clothes for a whole army of lazy hounds, who stuff and gorge themselves all day long, and half the night, and waste as much again as they eat; and to *pay* them once a quarter into the bargain, for letting themselves live at his expense and do nothing; pay them each as much as one of you can earn by working hard from sunrise to sunset.

20. Mind, he *must* do this. No matter what his inclination or disposition may be, he *must* keep up " a proper establishment." It is a " necessary" of his life. He would no more dare to do otherwise, than he would dare to let the parliament-men who sit for his boroughs vote according to their consciences. He is stingy enough where he dares to be so, heaven knows! and so do *you* know too, I dare say, if you have ever had to go into his servants' hall. I'll answer for it, all the strong ale you ever got there would have gone into a nutshell, without drowning the maggot that lodged in it. And if the beggar never

goes away empty handed from his door, it is
because he takes good care none shall ever get
near it.   And yet he *must* support this army of
menials, because he would not be " a Lord" without them.   It is they that *make* him " a nobleman," by *calling him one*.   If it were not for
them, neither he nor any one else would know
that he *was* one.

21. A " noble man," if it means any thing,
means something that is *better* than *us*, who
are of the common run of men.   And is *he*
this in himself? Look at his poor crazy carcass,
as it lolls back in its easy carriage to take the
air; and then tell me—Is there any thing in
that better than there is in yours, or in mine?
Does it look better? Can it act better? Can he
who owns it think better than we can, or talk
better? Is he more healthful, more honest, more
happy?   What can he *do* (of himself I mean)
that you or I cannot do as well, if not ten times
better?   In short, in what respect is he more of
A MAN than we are?   In what does he better,
or a tenth part so well, fulfil the objects of our
common existence?

22. " But look at his houses—his carriages
—his horses—his servants—his liveries"—you say.
Ay, there it is.   In *these* he *is* a " Lord;" and

consequently it is these that *make* him a Lord;
and *without* these he is none. These, therefore,
he *must* have, if they cost him half his income.
They are the " necessaries of life" of " a Lord."

22. In the next place, he must keep a pack of
hounds and a stable of hunters; though he does
not know a beagle from a bull-dog, or a fox from
a ferret, and is as little at home in his seat in the
saddle as he is in his seat in the House. He
must do this. What would *you* say of him if he
were to sell his dogs, and turn off his huntsmen,
and put his hunters into harness? What would
his *friends* say of him, who are kind enough
to come down from London every sporting season,
to ride those horses and follow those dogs, and
live through half the winter at his expense, to
save living at their own? What would his servants and country neighbours, the " gentry," and
substantial farmers (if there be any left) say of
him? What would he say and think and feel of
himself? Why that he was no longer " a Lord,"
to be sure; no longer what his ancestors were
before him, and what they made and left him.
He *must* do it. He has no choice.

23. Then this " Lord " has a " Lady;" and the
" Ladies" of " Lords," as every body knows, are
not the persons to *decrease* their expenses; for

if they *bring* them much, they take good care
to *spend* them more.   I believe, for my own part,
that this particular " Lord" of whom we are
speaking, would be glad enough to pass the rest
of his days quietly in the country; for he has
just sense enough to know that the racketings and
junketings of a London life have already left him
with " one foot in the grave ;" and he has too
lordly a fear of *death* to be in any hurry to help the
other there.   But the " Ladies" of Lords (especially when they are getting old) are not to be in-
fluenced by any fear of this sort. To do them justice,
they will have their swing, if they die for it,
and even *while* they are dying for it.   So long
as they can keep out of their coffins, they will
not keep out of their card-rooms, and ball-rooms.
And card-rooms and ball-rooms abroad beget
card-rooms and ball-rooms at home.   And for
this there must *be* a home.   And the " Home" of
the " Lady" of a great " Lord " means something
rather different from what you and I understand
by the word.   In short (for we have no time to
dwell upon it) it means much the same as the
" Home" of the " Lord " himself means in the
country; a place as big as a barrack ; plastered
over from top to bottom with paint and gilding ;
and beset at every step by another army of locusts,

in the shape of lacqueys, valets, butlers, footmen, coachmen, stablemen, housekeepers, lady's maids, housemaids, kitchen-maids, laundry-maids, and the Lord knows how many more besides : (not the " lord " of the house, by the bye ; for I'll be sworn *he* knows no more about the matter than if he had nothing to do with it. If he has been withinside half the rooms in his own house, and knows the name of a fourth part of his servants, it is as much as he does !)

24. This, then, is another " establishment" that is as much a " necessary of life" to a great " Lord," as bread and meat are to you and I. And the few " necessaries" that we have already seen go to the preserving of this " Lord's" life, must have swallowed up a pretty good slice of his income. But we have not seen half of them yet. You must know (for I'm sure you don't know it yet) that " people of fashion"—(and a " Lord " is always a person of fashion, by birth ; though in point of manners and habits he may be more vulgar than the boor that blacks his shoes) ; I say, " people of fashion" have decided among themselves, that it is altogether inconsistent with reason and common-sense, that they should live either in London or in the country, for more than about two-thirds of the year. " But if they live neither

E

in London nor in the country, where *are* they to
live?" you very naturally inquire.   Ay; that's
the question; and a pretty puzzling question it
is to them.   Quite as much so as it is to you.
But I'll tell you how they manage.

25. This habit, of not being able to live at
home during a certain portion of the year, has
long been prevalent among them; and they have
at last contrived (or at least those who gain a
base livelihood by administering to their idle,
senseless, and unnatural wants have contrived for
them) to establish certain spots, at a greater or less
distance from the WEN, and chiefly on the sea-
coast, but so situated in regard to soil, aspect,
&c. that nothing in the shape of vegetation will
flourish near them.   Now, where there is no vegetation there can evidently be no " Country."
Consequently these places (" watering-places"
they call them) bear no resemblance whatever to
either London or the Country, and are *therefore*
chosen as the residences of " people of fashion,"
during about a third part of every year.

26. But they do not build houses at these
places.   They *hire* them; hire them at an enormous expense, more than proportioned to that
of their own houses; while their own houses, and
all the " establishments" belonging to them, (or

nearly all), are going on just the same as if they themselves were there. Add to all this the expenses of getting backwards and forwards from these " watering-places," (which are the more fashionable the more expensive they are to reach) and we shall have got at another pretty hungry outlet for our " Lord's" income.

27. I fancy, if we calculate a little, we shall find that the forty thousand a year looks rather foolish by the time all these calls upon it have been answered. In fact, need I go any farther in my enumeration of the " necessaries" of a " Lord's" life? I think not. There are many " Lords" who cannot contrive to get these few " necessaries of life" which I have already named, with *double* the income of *our* lord. Not that they are therefore content to do without them. No —no—they continue to *get* them easily enough; but not with their income; not by paying for them honestly and fairly, as you and I are obliged to pay for whatever *we* get. They *get* them, it is true; but they get them " by hook and by crook," as the phrase goes; by means of a herd of rascally stewards, and attorneys, and money-lenders, and Jews; by mortgages, and postobits, and policies of insurance, and the devil of usury knows what

besides ; and by involving in comparative ruin
those who are to come after them, and who ought
by rights to receive the family estate bettered instead of beggared; and who do so receive it in
every case where the holder is an honest man.

28. Mind, I am not complaining of, or lament-
ing, this mode by which lords and people of fashion
" raise money," as they call it.   I should as soon
think of interfering, or feeling sorry, if I saw one
thief trying to pick another's pocket in the streets
of London.   I am not complaining of it ; I am
only telling you that so it is ; that this is what
many " Lords" are forced to do in order to keep
up those " establishments" which are necessary
to their existence ; and that among others my Lord
Lackwit is forced to do it.   And the consequence is that he does not enjoy a moment's
real peace of his lordly life, and that he cannot
honestly call the coat he wears his own.

29. And now comes the question with which
we began our inquiry about him.   *Is he a*
" RICH" *man?* Is this " Lord"—with his forty
thousand pounds a year, or three thousand three
hundred pounds a month, or eight hundred pounds
a week, or one hundred and ten pounds a day—
is he a " rich" man ?   Rich even in the mere

money of which alone we are now speaking? I will not insult your understandings by answering the question.

30. Now let us give a look back at the other part of the inquiry, as to who is properly to be called a " poor" man; still confining the question to money alone, and still keeping in mind the principle on which we set out, that a man is " rich," or " poor," in proportion as he has *much,* or *less than nothing,* left, after having supplied himself and his family with what are, to them, " the necessaries of life "

31. When I lived at Botley, there was (and I hope still is) an honest labourer, named Will Grange, who rented the little cottage at the corner of the lane as you turn down to the Holt. Every body at Botley knew Will Grange. He used to work for me; and I was proud to see him in my fields. He was a credit to any master: if indeed it is not a piece of impudent presumption for any man to call himself the " master" of another, merely because that other chooses, of his own free will, to do certain things, for a certain price which is fixed upon beforehand. If a labourer, of no matter what description, does the work for me that I require and engage him to do, and that he agrees to do, I *must* pay him the price of his

labour. I have no *choice* in the matter. I *must* do it ; for if I refuse to do it by fair means, he can *make* me do it. Thank heaven, we have still *so much* of justice left in our debased and degraded country. When he has done his day's work he can *make* me pay him the price of it, and need never do another for me while he lives, unless he *likes*. What impudence, then, for me to call myself the *master* of this man ! And what abject baseness in him, to call and to consider himself as my *slave!* For the word " master" is without a meaning, except when coupled with that other word, " *slave*."

32. But to return to honest Will Grange, who, if I remember rightly, never called any man " master" ; though he was as far from fancying himself *above* his station as he was from feeling himself *below* it. Will Grange, when I knew him, was a labourer ; a day labourer. I need not tell *you* that this means, one who earns his livelihood, day by day, by the sweat of his brow. He had been this all his life ; and at the time I am speaking of he had been this long enough to have enabled him to get together just enough to purchase a cow and the furniture of the cottage in which he lived. He had, when I last saw him, a wife and four children.

33. Now what would my Lord Lackwit, or any other "Lord," or any of the herds of "nobility and gentry," as they call themselves, who live upon the plunder that comes out of the pockets of the oppressed people of this degraded country ; what would any of these "gentry" say, if you were to ask them seriously whether a man like Will Grange, a day labourer, with a wife and four children to support out of the earnings of that labour, is a "poor" man or a "rich" one ? What would they say ? Why they would *say* nothing ; but they would first laugh in your face, and then turn away their heads in token of their contempt for the person who could ask them such a silly question. And they would do just the same if you were to ask them whether my Lord Lackwit is a "rich" man.

34. But does this *make* or *prove* the Lord to be in reality "rich" and the labourer "poor?" Heaven forbid ! If any thing that *they* could either think or say could alter the condition of their "inferiors," (as they are pleased to term *us* who *do* something for our bread,) we should all of us be rather worse off than we are at present : which, heaven knows, need not be. But *is* Will Grange a "poor" man ? for I will suppose that

he still is what he was when I knew him.   Let us see.

35. I have said that he lives in a snug little cottage, large enough to afford a warm shelter to all his family in the winter weather : in the summer they want none. I have said also that he has a cow.   This he keeps, partly by letting the youngest of his little ones lead it in a string about the green lanes ; (for there is no common in his neighbourhood); but *chiefly* by the produce of the forty rods, or thereabouts, of garden ground which is attached to his cottage.   This ground he cultivates entirely with a view to the keep of his cow ; because he has the good sense to know, that by so doing he contributes more towards the health and comfort of his wife and children, than if he could fill it ten times over with potatoes and " garden stuff."

36. The cabbages and turnips that will grow in this forty rods of land feed his cow well and plentifully during the whole winter, and all that part of the summer when she cannot pick up her living in the lanes and by the road side. And while she is well fed his children never want a bowl of good wholesome skimmed milk ; and his wife can make as much butter with the cream

that comes from it, as will give an increase to their weekly earnings, at least equal to what two additional days' work in the week would do.

37. He is able to cultivate this bit of ground easily, by taking an hour now and then before and after his ordinary day's work, and by the assistance of his eldest boy; to say nothing of his having all *Sunday* to himself: and theirs must be an odd kind of *religion* who would object to his employing a portion of that day, " holy" as it is, to such an end : for what work can be holier, I should be glad to know, than that which contributes to the health and comfort of the offspring which God has given him?

38. This cow, which, observe, is almost entirely kept by the labour of honest Will, and which must therefore be looked upon in the light of the actual consequence of that labour, is the only direct source of profit which he possesses, exclusive of his own daily earnings. So that he is not to be considered as any other than an ordinary day labourer. Mind this ; because it is of consequence to my argument that you should not regard Will Grange, my *example* in this case, as any other than a common labourer, like one of yourselves.

39. But Will has a wife ; a good, honest, comely, industrious, neat-handed wife. And in

no station of life, and least of all in *yours*, can a man be all that he *may* be in that station, *without* such a wife; any more than he can be it *with* one of an opposite description ; with a slattern, a scold, and a gossip : for these precious qualities always go together.

40. Now Will's wife, as every good wife ought, (I had almost said as every good wife *does* ; but I'm afraid this would be going a little too far, considering that not more than about sixty thousand copies of my Cottage Economy have as yet been circulated), I say that Will's wife hates and abhors all manner of slops and messes about the cottage ; and most of all she hates that worst, because most mischievous of all messes, tea.

41. As for the children, they do not know the taste of beer, much less of any thing stronger. And what little of it Will himself may stand in need of, to enable him to get through his daily labour more cheerfully, they can afford to buy : that is if they *can* buy such a thing as beer at all now-a-days, or get it any way without *making* it themselves.   I'm afraid that, at the time we are speaking of, this excellent custom of brewing at home ; this custom so indispensable to the English cottager's enjoying the greatest share of health and comfort of which his station is susceptible ;

was almost necessarily laid aside, in consequence
of the monstrous weight of taxes which had been
laid on all the materials of brewing; and which
custom, by the bye, I do not despair of seeing
almost universally revived at no very distant
day, when the cottagers shall have read and considered what I have written for them, on this most
important subject, in my Cottage Economy. But
we will suppose that Will Grange did not, because under the then circumstances of the times
he could not, brew their own beer. All that they
needed they could well afford to buy, out of the
earnings of their cow.

42. Then for bread, *that* of course Will's wife
baked herself. If she had not, I should never
have called her an " industrious" wife; no, not
even an " honest" one; for a cottager's wife who
chooses to feed her children upon the pernicious
trash that she gets at the bakers for about half
as much again as she can make good wholesome
bread herself, has no more claim to be called
" honest," than any one has who defrauds others
of what is their due. The married labourer's earnings are in part the *due* of his children; for if
it were not for them he would not take the trouble
of earning so much as he does. That mother,
then, who squanders away those earnings unne-

cessarily (to say nothing of mischievously) *robs* her children of their due. This is what Will's wife never did, or I should not now be offering him and his family as an example to illustrate the point of inquiry that we are presently coming to.

43. I must not dwell much longer on the *details* connected with this point; and I need not. It is sufficient to say that the inmates of Will Grange's cottage have seldom occasion *to go elsewhere* in search of any thing that they may want to make their lives easy, and even cheerful and happy. They have a few pigs of course; which, with good management, not only give them bacon for every alternate day throughout the year, but, together with the cow, afford them plenty of manure for their little garden; without an ample supply of which they could not get from it what I have said that they do get; namely, food for the cow during nine months out of the twelve. They have also half a dozen laying hens, which always afford them a *hot* dinner, when the cupboard happens to run bare. And they have a couple of hives of bees, which give them honey enough for the younger children always to have a scrape of it upon their hunch of bread, before they go to bed.

44. This is *all* that Will Grange and his family have within themselves, to be sure. But then what an "ALL" it is! I should like to see the "LORD" who is half so independent of the rest of the world, as this honest labourer, and his industrious, healthy, and happy family; who may almost be considered as the *creators* of all that is necessary to supply their daily wants, and who have nearly the whole of their earnings left, to buy themselves and their children decent and comfortable clothing, and to lay by for a rainy day.

45. It is true that, after supplying themselves with all the comforts which any of us require, they have not enough left to pay for their children going to school to the parson of the parish, to be taught to spurn at their station, and be ashamed of the father that fed, and the mother that bore them. It is true they have not surplus enough to let them sit at home idle half their time, and quarrel with one another to make it pass away the more quickly; or if they like that better, the husband to loll at the alehouse and get drunk three days in the week, while the wife leaves the children at home to "mind" each other, and goes gadding about through the village, tea-drinking, trolloping, and tale-bearing.

46. It is true they have not enough to tempt

them to do these things, and half a hundred
more, equally proper and praiseworthy, which a
superfluity *might* tempt even them to do, because it *has* before now tempted others, who,
without that temptation, would have been as
honest and as happy as *they* are.   But, as we
have just seen, they have enough and to spare
for all the *good* purposes to which money can be
applied in their station of life ; a station which,
if it were what it *might be* from its nature, and
what it *ought to be* according to the claims of
natural justice, would be the envy of all other
stations, and the glory and delight of all who
belong to it.

47. And now our question returns : Is Will
Grange a " poor" man ?   Again let me say, I will
not insult your understandings by answering this
question ; because I am sure that you have already
answered it for yourselves, and answered it in a
way that will I hope make it quite needless for
me to advise you to give up all those idle crotchets
that I hear you have got into your heads, about
leaving your beautiful, healthful, and sweet-scent-
ed fields, and coming up to " seek your fortunes"
in this detestable sink of all filth, folly, and
iniquity ; this standing and ever-increasing disease
of our country ; this WEN ; this London.   Shun

it, my honest friends, as you would shun a pest-house, or a parish work-house. You may take my word for it, that all the " fortune" you, with your habits, could ever find in London, would be poverty, contempt, and shame. By the bye, if you knew what London is, I need not have named the two last; for *there* poverty *means* them both.

48. But even if you were sure of earning, by coming here, three times as much as you can by remaining where you are, you would be still three times as badly off, because you would, in a month from the time you set foot in this want-creating city, have ten times as many to supply as you now have, besides losing the power of enjoying that supply even if you could get it. No, no, my good friends; stay where you are, and be as contented as you can till better times come. And come they must, one way or another; and that shortly. In the mean while you may believe me when I tell you, that the only " rich" man is he who is healthy, honest, and contented with his lot; (neither of which *anybody* is in London); and that the only " poor" man is he who has wants that he cannot supply.

So says your sincere friend
And well-wisher,
WILLIAM COBBETT.

Kensington, Sep. 1825.

TO-MORROW;

A GAIETY AND GRAVITY.

ONE OF THE AUTHORS OF " REJECTED ADDRESSES."

TO-MORROW;

A GAIETY AND GRAVITY.

BY ONE OF THE AUTHORS OF " REJECTED ADDRESSES."

" To-morrow, and to-morrow, and to-morrow."
MACBETH.

IT seems but yesterday that I took occasion to bestow a month's immortality upon " To-day;" and I propose not to let To-day pass without doing as much for To-morrow. Perhaps I may devote To-morrow to performing a similar office for Yesterday. But this latter is more than I can promise, since it is the very essence of To-morrow that no one can tell what it will bring forth.

Of all the days in the year, there is none so pregnant of wise determinations, flattering promises, sage resolutions, and salutary reforms, as To-morrow. It is astonishing what projects are to be commenced To-morrow; and it is still more sur-

prising what a number are to be brought to a conclusion on the same day !

Judging from the innumerable tradesmen's bills
that are to be paid " To-morrow," one would suppose that some new source of wealth had been simul-
taneously discovered by every small debtor throughout the world of crédit, and that to pay were as
easy and agreeable as to run in debt.

As for the intended " calls " of To-morrow, if
they should all be made they will all be to make
over again ; for every body will be out calling, on
every body.   Then again, the " new leaves " that
are to be " turned over " To-morrow, are more
numerous than those " in Valombrosa's shade."

In short, To-morrow is to be the day more " big
with fate " than any that the sun ever shone upon ;
and more is to be done in the course of it than has
been done in any day since the world was made
out of chaos.   And, " not to speak it profanely,"
even on *that* day there was but form and entity
given to what was before a confused mass of
matter ; whereas To-morrow, thoughts, intentions,
fancies, feelings, and imaginations, are to be me-
tamorphosed into actual and tangible facts ; and
what is more, a thousand events are to take place
that will never take place at all !

What a world would this be, if' all were accomplished in it that assuredly *will* be accomplished to-morrow! To-morrow A. will ask a friend to dine with him; and B. will be as good as his word; and C. will commit no blunder; and D. will get a decision in the Court of Chancery; and E. will commence his new epic; and F. will finish his; and G. will begin to grow wise; and H. will begin to grow honest; and I. will begin to leave off writing nonsense; and K. will keep himself sober; and L. will not tell a single lie; and M. will try to make himself agreeable; and N. will not; and O. will get over his own style; and P. will pay his long-standing tailor's bill; and Q. will quarrel with a taller man than himself; and R. will begin to retrench his expences within his income; and S. will say a good thing; and T. will tell one without spoiling it; and V. will vote in opposition to his interest; and U. will read this essay a second time; and W. will leave off wondering who wrote it; and X. Y. Z. will get a satisfactory answer to his advertisement for a wife.

And why is it that all these good things, and a thousand more, which will certainly take place To-morrow, never take place at all? The secret is, that To-morrow, like " good bye," is easily said,

and that most of us are content to let our good
deeds appear under the guise of good words.

Besides which, though every body talks and
thinks of To-morrow as of a day that must come,
and though it is as familiar in our mouths " as
household words," yet we all feel that it is *only*
a word—that there is no such thing as To-morrow
—that it is a day which cannot happen—a *dies
non.* Who can explain what To-morrow is?—or
where it is?—or when it is? It is always coming,
like a waiter at an inn; and yet it never comes.
The little boys at school understand it best. They
call it " To-morrow come-never."

And probably *this*, after all, is the point of
view in which most people secretly look at To-
morrow. And, accordingly, they are willing to
do anything in the world to oblige you—"To-
morrow." "To-day" they really must be excused
—they have so many things to attend to—but if
you will but call To-morrow——. And then, when
you fancy that "To-morrow" is come, and you take
them at their word—Oh, they really can't find
time To-day—but "To-morrow." And then when
that To-morrow comes—they are really very sorry
—but " circumstances have transpired," &c. And
thus it goes on for ever :

" To-morrow, and to-morrow, and to-morrow
Creeps in this petty pace from day to day,
To the last syllable of recorded time;
And all our yesterdays have lighted fools
(and wise men too)
The way to "——To-morrow!

An ancient philosopher has said, that he is wise who has lived To-day. And it was wisely said. And his commentator has added, no less wisely, that he is wiser still who lived Yesterday. Let me, who am albeit neither philosopher nor commentator, not be accused of presumption, if I complete the trinity of wise saying, by adding, that he is wisest of the three who lives To-morrow; for To-morrow we may live as we please, whether it comes to us or not.

In truth, we have hitherto been considering this subject with a degree of flippancy which is scarcely appropriate to it; for after all, what is To-morrow but that great Future to which we all look, and to which we are all hastening, on the swift pinions of Time, and must inevitably reach, even though we should succeed in trifling away To-day as we did Yesterday, and To-morrow as we have done To-day. The only truly wise man, is he who so passes To-day, that To-morrow may be

anticipated if it come not, and improved and enjoyed if it come.

In the present frightfully artificial and diseased
state of society—with its ever-increasing cities,
and its ever more and more deserted and despised
fields, and groves, and solitudes;—when all are
rushing towards the plague-tainted spots, and
crowding into them as if they were tired of health,
and in love with disease and death;—when govern-
ments are going about, under the guise of *holi-
ness*, seeking whom among the weak and dis-
united they may devour, and among the virtuous
divide and destroy;—when rulers are raking in the
dirt of ages for pleas and precedents, whereby
they may debase the people they have been put
over, and lay their liberty prostrate at the feet of
power;—in short, when vice, luxury, and crime
(to say nothing of cant, cajolery, and cunning)
reign triumphant; and virtue, wisdom, and nature are laughed to scorn, and driven to seek
refuge in the solitudes of woods and deserts—
what should the truly wise man do, but live in
that only world which is left him unpolluted, and
of which he can make what use he pleases, by
fashioning it after any form that his fancy feels
inclined to—namely, the world of To-morrow—the

great Future—" the all hailed hereafter?" Let me ask those who doubt the wisdom of living with a view to To-morrow rather than To-day,— Of what avail were all the riches which Crœsus looked upon as the prime blessing of life—or the honour which was so honoured by Periander of Corinth—or the strength which Milo the Crotonian boasted of—or the knowledge which Socrates worshipped—or the beauty which Orpheus adored —or the ideal world of Plato—or the prudence and forethought of Thales the Milesian—or even the supreme virtue to which Aristotle referred all happiness, and the happiness itself which Epicurus alone thought worth living for—what were all these, unless with a view to To-morrow?

Would any one consent even to live through To-day, if he were sure that no To-morrow would follow it? Alas! To-morrow is not a matter to be trifled either with or upon. It is the best part of our existence; since it is the only part of which we can be sure that it *will* be what we would *have it be*. Ophelia says that " we all know what we are, but we know not what we may be." But with all due deference to the wisdom of her simplicity, she was wrong in both clauses of her proposition. None of us know what we *are*; and we all know what we may be

—To-morrow ; because To-morrow itself is but an imagination ; and while we are imagining *it*, we can just as well imagine ourselves into what we please when it arrives. True, it arrives at last ; and then we do not find either it or ourselves what we intended or expected them to be. But then it cannot be said that we have deceived ourselves ; because we cannot find out our error till *to-day ;* and then To-morrow is before us again, as fresh and promising as ever.

In a word, those who would live to any good end in the present unnatural and over-excited state of society and manners, (to say nothing of the corruption in morals and the degradation in politics), must make up their minds to forget Yesterday, and take no note of To-day, but live in the future of To-morrow : for in the wise man's calendar there are but these three days, which include all time, past, present, and to come.

But *can* they so live ? Can the unavailing Yesterday be forgotten, and the imaginary To-morrow be enjoyed, amidst the feverish turmoil and the insane noise and distraction of To-day, as it exists in the centre and heart of society and the world ? Assuredly not. But " there is another and a better world"—the world of woods, and fields, and gardens, and groves, and streams—each department of which is a world of itself, and peopled with beings who live only to be happy, and who are happy only that they live. In *that* world the soul may find rest for its wearied wings, and refreshment for its exhausted powers ; there it may contemplate the future with a quiet and undisturbed gaze, till at last it sinks softly into it, and becomes a part of what it looks upon.

There are many other points of view in which To-morrow may be looked upon ; but I fear the reader will be of opinion that I have said more than enough of it for To-day. At any rate, I have exhausted my limits, if not my subject ; and the remaining considerations touching To-morrow,must be deferred till—To-morrow.

H.

DEMONIACALS.

(POSTHUMOUS.)

BY CHILDE HAROLDE.

G

THE TOKEN.

To ———

LADY, forbear the fruitless strife !
Would'st thou forget this solemn Token ?
It may not be ! this holds thy life
In bonds, that never can be broken.

This consummated the deep vow
Breathed at the marriage of our minds ;
And by its power I claim thee now :——
The silent spell thy spirit binds.

I claim THEE :——not thine outward beauty——
That lost for ever its controul
When thy thoughts wandered from their duty :——
But THEE——thy mind and heart and soul.

How I once loved them !   Human love
Was never felt more deeply pure ;
But 'twas an effluence from above,
That could not—ought not to endure.

It was too spiritually bright
To mingle with a form of earth,
Even tho' that form of seeming light
Belied the dungeon of its birth,

And breathed of heaven.—One fatal hour
Hath changed all hours to come.   Love's fled,
And with it love-born bliss :—the flower
Must wither when its root is dead.

But not the less I claim *thy* faith :
Unsought—unhoped for it was given :
Witness the listening earth beneath—
The watching stars—the breathing heaven.

That deep-vowed faith thou canst recall
Never !—this simple ring of gold
To thee is magical—its thrall
Holds thee, and shall not cease to hold.

Then struggle not—no force of thine
Can break the bond—no art can sever
Its links of adamant—thou'rt mine,
Absent or present—now—for ever!

REMONSTRANCE.

TO THE SAME.

PAUSE! pause and listen! 'Tis a voice
That *was* all music to thine ear ;—
Now hear its deep-breath'd discords!   Pause-
Listen, and think, and fear !

Thy hopes stand trembling on the brink
Of a dark stream not to be cross'd ;
One plunge, and they for ever sink !
Turn back—or thou art lost.

Who hath done this ?—With impious force
   To tear the spirit from its shrine,
And call it *marriage* !—'Tis divorce !
   Thy heart and soul are mine !

Need I recall that solemn hour?
Alas! it *will* not be forgot.
'Twas brief and silent—but its power
Hath fix'd thy future lot.

Silent and brief—but its deep bliss,
Though fatal now, cannot decay:
The memory of that first—last kiss,
Shall never pass away.

Passion can work strange ends—a trance
Comes over me—it stills my pain.
What! tears!—ay—let them flow!—perchance
You ne'er may smile again.

Passion can work strange ends: I hear
Accents, that seem to have their birth
In the deep prophetic heart.—Revere
Sounds that are not of earth!

" Dare not to struggle against fate!
" Or, with a guilty weakness, yield
" To bonds that shall lay desolate
" The path thy youth revealed!

" Else shall the merry bridal bell
" Ring out a death-peal to thy joy ;
" And every hope that fatal knell
" Shall kill—but not *destroy :*

" Their ghosts shall linger with thee yet,
" Telling a tale of future years
" That shall thy bridal pillow wet
" With unavailing tears.

" When thy friends wish thee " Joy !"—the word
" Shall sound like mockery to thine ear ;
' And its dim echo haunt thy thoughts
" Like a perpetual fear.

" But last, and most of all, beware
" The bridal kiss :—*that* seals thy doom ;
" Changing so foul what else were fair—
" A temple to a tomb.

" *That* renders even repentance vain ;—
" For as thy last faint smiles depart,
" A cold, dull, everlasting pain
" Shall settle at thy heart !"

STANZAS.

TO THE SAME.

I DREAD to think upon thy fate,
Yet all my thoughts *will* that way tend :
Forms of the Past they recreate,
And with the Future blend.

Love consecrates the marriage bed ;
Without it all is guilt and gloom ;
A living form linked to a dead !—
A spirit in a tomb !

Better be senseless dust indeed,—
Of the vile flesh-worm's food a part,—
Than live to pamper worms that feed
Upon the *living* heart.

To die is nothing ; but to feel
A living death creep thro' thy veins,
While hope yet lingers, not to heal,
But aggravate thy pains ;—

This is to neither live nor die—
Suffering at one the worst of both.———
What desperate hope starts to thine eye ?-
Beware !—thy bridal oath !

Besides—I only *pity* thee :
Thy guilty weakness lost my *love*.
On earth thou hast nowhere to flee !
No hope—but " Heaven above ! !"

DINING OUT.

BY " ONE OF THE AUTHORS OF REJECTED ADDRESSES.

DINING OUT.

BY " ONE OF THE AUTHORS OF REJECTED ADDRESSES."

DINING OUT is an accomplishment in which we English do not excel. It demands a certain politic pliancy, both of mind and body, which we cannot boast. It is that one among the Fine Arts in which we are immeasurably behind our continental neighbours. In fact we are the worst Diners-out in the world. We do not understand the principle of it. Even the South Sea Islanders understand and practice it better ; for when *they* go to a dinner party, it is for the express purpose of dining upon an enemy ; whereas an Englishman, when he does not dine at home, dines upon his friend. The truth is, that in civilized society, Dining out has nothing whatever to do with eating and drinking. Who asks a man to dine out that cannot afford to dine at home ?—The thing never

happened.   It is altogether incompatible with the
" scope and tendency" of dinner parties.

Not that one can dine out *without* eating and
drinking.   But for that very reason, among others,
eating and drinking are but secondary consequences
of Dining Out, and are no causes of it at all.   They
are necessary concomitants of it, to be sure; just
as tea accompanies talk in a party of elderly ladies,
and as love goes hand in hand (for a little way)
with marriage, in a youthful pair, of opposite sexes.
But eating and drinking have no more to do with
the immediate end of Dining Out, than love has
to do with that of marriage, or marriage with that
of love.

In England, there is nothing to be done, or
even undertaken, without a dinner party.   From
the governing of the nation to the goings on of
the pettiest of its parishes, all begins and all ends
in a dinner.   Accordingly, there is no country in
which dinner parties assume so pleasing a variety
as they do here.   We have dinners on all occasions,—from the Coronation of the King, to the
Christening of the newest born of his subjects;
dinners in all places,—from the palaces of the
peers in Saint James's, to the *buck-slums* of the
beggars in Saint Giles's; dinners of all dimen-
sions,—from the calipash and calipee of the

cabinet minister, to the *pot-luck* of the cabinet maker. We have dinners of all denominations : diplomatic dinners, and patriotic dinners, and pugilistic dinners, and parliamentary dinners ; cabinet dinners and reform dinners : ministerial dinners and opposition dinners ; O. P. dinners and P. S. dinners ; Pitt dinners and Fox dinners ; election dinners, and theatrical dinners, and literary dinners, and scientific dinners.——Is a minister to be ousted from his place ? The cabal is concocted and carried on at a dinner party. Is a million to be raised by a joint-stock company, in order that certain clerks and projectors may be able to dine in private ?——They must first assemble the intended sufferers at a dinner in public.——Is a chapel to be built, a charity founded, a school formed, an institution established ?——Ask the public to dinner, and it is done.——Does a friend want to borrow fifty pounds of you ?——He asks you to dine with him at a tavern, and pays the bill with your own money.——Even Mr. Owen cannot banish vice from the world without the aid of a public dinner——(nor with one either.) Nay——marriages themselves——which are elsewhere " made in heaven" ——are here made at a dinner party arranged for the purpose !

All this admitted, one would expect that John

Bull, being so used to it, would make an excellent Diner-out. As we have happily had opportunities of meeting him at nearly all the different kinds of dinner parties above alluded to,—as well as at numerous others " too tedious to mention," as the conjurors' advertisements have it,—we may perhaps occasionally introduce the reader to some of them, and enable him to judge for himself. And if he should object to this, that Dining Out in imagination is likely to afford but " lenten entertainment," he may be assured that it will be our fault if the reflection is not pleasanter to look upon than the reality : for it must be a very handsome face indeed that does not look better in a mirror than out of it.

The dinner party to which we now invite our friends shall be one of that class which is perhaps of all others the most characteristically English. The family of the Tibbs's move in the first circles of city life : in other words, they are never to be seen in the city at all, except when they pay an occasional visit of ceremony to Saint Mary Axe, or " dine out" once in the season or so, at Devonshire Square: for they would not be thought proud, though they do reside near the Regent's Park!—The family consists, in the male branch, of Mr. Tibbs and his son Thomas. Mr. T. the elder

is a person " engaged in mercantile pursuits," as
his wife and daughters delicately phrase it ; but
according to his own less ambiguous and ambitious version of the matter, he is a Manchester ware-
houseman.   To say that he was formerly a " ware-
houseman" merely, without the " Manchester,"
and *that* in the very concern which he now owns,
is to describe him as at once shrewd, upright, and
not altogether without either pride, or prejudices.
Mr. Tibbs the elder has a son and heir, who, in
virtue of this latter quality in particular, is allowed
the privilege of persuading himself that he has a
soul altogether incapable of admitting the idea of
printed muslins, and which holds brown holland in
a natural abhorrence. Accordingly, he has received
the best education that Dr. Drill could prevail
upon him to accept, and is now near the end of
his term in an attorney's office.

The female Tibbs's are more numerous than the
males, and not less worthy of historical mention.
We must, however, touch upon the merits of each
but very slightly, or we shall not be in time to
assist at their dinner party.   Mrs. Tibbs is by
no means " of a certain age :" which is saying,
in other words, that she *is* of a very certain age,
and doesn't care who knows it.   She is moreover

H

unaffectedly fond of her children ; so that there is nothing in the shape of rivalry between them. But she is fond of herself too ; for she is in the habit of cherishing a very natural notion, that, if one sets the example of not loving oneself, it would be strange indeed if others did not follow it ; seeing that we ourselves must necessarily be the best possible judges of our own deserts. The best of Mrs. Tibbs's self-love is, however, that she is apt to consider her husband and children, and even her house and furniture, as part and parcel of herself, and is satisfied that in admiring them you are admiring her. It must be confessed, in passing, that in this Mrs. T. is more philosophical than she is aware of : for to philosophy she makes no pretensions whatever, and thinks that in the family of an English merchant it would be altogether out of place.

Mrs. Tibbs has three daughters ; Juliana and Frances, who, being women grown, Mrs. Tibbs considers as entitled to be called " the girls ;" and Jessica—who being born five years after the youngest of the others, is destined to remain " the child" till her sisters cease to be " the girls." The said " girls" are, in their own house and their own opinion, considered as very *fine* young women :

which epithet, being interpreted, signifies that
they are somewhat *coarse*. In fact, their Irish ad-
mirer (for he professedly admires them both at
present) Captain Castabout, is fain to confess
that their forms are constructed on a scale of con-
siderable magnitude, and that their ruddy complexions indicate a degree of health amounting to
what is rudely enough denominated *rude :* so much
so, indeed, that Miss Priscilla Paleface, who re-
sides on the opposite side of the Place, cannot
abide to stand at the window when they go out :
she says they *look as if* they were painted, without
being so ; which she thinks extremely vulgar at
best—not to say indecent.

In regard to the mental qualities and accom-
plishments of the two elder Miss Tibbs's—or as
the boards at the young ladies' seminaries insist
on having it, the Misses Tibbs—we have but
little to report at present. Suffice it that they
speak French with a propriety of accent peculiar
to English young ladies who have visited Paris ;
know enough of Italian to be able to explain
to Captain C. (who never fails to make the inquiry) that " *Ah ! perdona,*" means " I beg your
pardon ;" play the piano with a perseverance that
is truly praiseworthy, and a spirit that some of
their hearers characterize by the epithet which, as

H 2

we have hinted above, others apply to their appearance of health ; and sing Moore's melodies in a highly decorous style : by which latter we would be understood to indicate that their execution of these very " taking airs" is in no degree calculated to endanger the morals of their hearers. Finally, Juliana, the eldest Miss Tibbs, may, by particular entreaty, be occasionally prevailed upon to bestow her embraces on one of Erard's harps ; which process she is accustomed to accomplish in so edifying a fashion, that Captain C., who is generally present on these occasions, never fails to turn round to his next male neighbour once or twice during the exhibition, and favour him with a knowing look, which the other, unless he happens to be an Irishman, can seldom be prevailed upon to understand.

It only remains to speak of little Jessica ; for though she is still ranked as a school-girl at home, she has left school nominally, and is therefore entitled to a permanent place in our family picture. And yet we are half disposed to leave her out altogether ; since she is not exactly in keeping with any other part of it.   Let us pass her over slightly, by saying that she is one of those plants which are occasionally found to spring up, as if spontaneously, in a soil and under circumstances altogether uncongenial to them, or at least altogether unlikely to have produced them according to the common course of things. She reminds one of a lily of the valley in the midst of a bed of poppies, or a delicate *white* rose starting from the same root with a whole family of flaunting red ones. There is a natural refinement about the little Jessica—both of mind, manner, and person—which has in fact no connexion whatever with place or circumstances; and into the causes of which we are not in a mood sufficiently philosophical to penetrate, even if this were a fit occasion. Suffice it therefore to add that Jessica, " the gentle Jessica," was born a few days after her mama had been to see the Merchant of Venice, and received her name from the association of ideas attendant on that circumstance. This is the only touch of the romantic that can be detected in the history of the Tibbs's.

Be it known that Mr. and Mrs. Tibbs are above the affectation of assembling all their friends once or twice in a season to a crowded " At Home," and treating them to thin negus, miscellaneous biscuits, and a seat between six;—for they shrewdly suspect that the said practice is no less dictated by the parsimony of the inviters, than they know it to be destructive to the

pleasure of the invited.   They have no notion that
any thing is worth having, and therefore worth
offering, that *costs* nothing ; and as they can
afford it, they never ask people to sit upon any
other chairs than their own.   It is to one of the
dinner parties which grew out of this prejudice
(which, by the by, the most fastidious of their
friends admit to be an amiable one) that we shall
now introduce our readers.   As, however, we have
not hitherto had any cause to indulge in a pique
against the said readers, we shall spare them the
trouble of forming one of the party as it remains
assembled in the drawing-room during the half
hour following that named in the *invite:* for if
there be an occasion when the genii of awkward-
ness and ennui take incarnate forms, and each
multiplies itself by eight, like Kehama, it is at
a party of sixteen assembled as aforesaid.   We
will therefore join the Tibbs's party at the foot
of the stairs, and enter the dining-room with it
at once.

In ten minutes (and not less) the company were
seated to the satisfaction of Mrs. T.,—who always
insists on managing these matters herself, and
utterly sets her face against that freewill which
she hears is making such alarming encroachments
in the realms of fashion : for she is of Lady Mac-

beth's opinion, that " the sauce to meat is ceremony." She thinks too, with the same hostess,
that

> " ———————————the feast is sold
> That is not often vouch'd, while 'tis a making,
> 'Tis given with welcome."

Accordingly, she expresses that welcome occasionally during *her* feasts ; to the great scandal of
her son Thomas, who has imbibed notions which
she considers of a very heterodox nature in these
particulars ; and to the infinite horror on this occasion of Miss Leftoff, the antiquated sister in law
of a city knight, at whose house in Nottingham
Place she occasionally dines, and whose fashionable
friends, she will venture to say, never made any
body welcome in their lives ! It need scarcely be
intimated that Miss L. took the precaution of expressing this opinion by looks alone.

Of the cates that displayed themselves on re-
moving the spacious cushion-shaped covers (for
the Tibbs's have not yet escaped from the Age of
Tin in this particular) we shall not give any minute
account ; merely stating that they maintained a
well-poised medium between the mere substantials,
clad *au naturel*, of the old English school, and the
" high fantasticals" of the modern French *cuisine*

—that Monmouth-street of meats—where they get
dressed out in a hundred different fashions of se-
cond-hand frippery, in not one of which do their
best friends know them.

Dinner now commenced, and taciturnity began
at the same moment to sound a retreat. For an
Englishman, if he will talk at no other time, will
at his dinner. He then sees something before
him to talk about : which at other times he is
forced to imagine ; and that is too much trouble :
—for, whatever his friends or enemies may say to
the contrary, John Bull is the most *poco-curante*
animal in nature, and cares for nothing that does
not " come home to his *business*."—But let us
have no digressions *from* our dinner, whatever we
may be obliged to endure *at* it.

Mrs. Tibbs had taken the precaution, as in duty
to her good dinner bound, of arranging the male
portion of her company with an eye to what her
covers concealed ; so that when they disappeared,
each party found himself opposite to the dish best
adapted to his dissecting talents. For the first
ten minutes, therefore, after the removal of the
accustomed soup and fish which never failed to
form the standing top and bottom of the Tibbs's
table, nothing was distinguishable but a somewhat
confused hubbub, consisting of the heads and tails

of phrases as disjointed as the contents of the
dishes to which they referred—such as " May I
be permitted ——" " Will you allow me ——"
" Really I'm quite ashamed ——" " Pray give
me leave ——" " I'm sorry to trouble you ——"
" The trouble's a pleasure——" &c. &c. &c. By
the bye, we should not have permitted the aforesaid soup and fish to have entirely vacated their
places, without repeating an enormous pun appertaining thereto, which Mr. Tibbs the younger had
picked up at office that morning, and being a bit
of a wag, perpetrated on this occasion. And we
are the more unwilling that it should be defrauded
of its fame, seeing that the youth had magnanimity
enough to mulct himself of both soup and fish, in
order to have an opportunity of atcheiving it.
Both Mr. and Mrs. T. happened to ask him, nearly
at the same moment, which he would chuse, soup
or fish ; to which he replied, " with infinite promp-
titude," that he did not chuse either, for that
he was not *a superficial* person. This sally,
though it greatly scandalized Mr. Tibbs, the elder,
and fell entirely still-born on the ear of Mrs. T.,
was received by the company in general with great
eclat ; and moreover it had the important effect of
deciding the future fate of Mr. Deputy Double-
chin's youngest son—which had been resting in

equilibrio for the last six months, and which was now finally fixed for an attorney's office—" it made a lad so sharp," the Deputy said.

We must now let the dinner take its course till the sweets come on; for the remarks of city epicures on the merits of any *given* dish are only edifying when the dish itself happens to be at hand, and the hearer can prove the truth of the dogma laid down in regard to it.   Suffice it that the gentlemen had all " great pleasure in taking wine" with each other, and that each of the ladies bowed their heads sundry times across the table, in token of their skill in practising the ingenious fiction of doing the same without wetting their lips : for ladies in the class of those with whom we have at present the pleasure of associating, (especially unmarried ones,) have a notion that they are bound to take wine with every body who asks them, and are at the same time bound to avoid taking wine at all, as studiously as if they were Mussulmans.   A young lady from the city, who should be detected in taking two glasses of wine at dinner, would expect her father's clerk to make love to her the next day, and would not be very angry if he did.

Towards the latter end of a dinner-party, if at all, an Englishman begins to feel a disposition to hear himself talk. Accordingly, then it was that

the topics of the day began to be discussed at the
table of the Tibbs's. And who, after having been
present at a party of this kind, shall say that business and politics are the only subjects in which
Englishmen of the middle classes take an interest,
and that literature, and the fine arts, do not enjoy
their due share of consideration? On the present
occasion Mrs. Tibbs herself introduced the subject
of literature even before the cloth was drawn, by
observing that she understood from her girls Sir
Walter Scott's last new play of Woodstock was not
near so clever as two that he wrote some time ago
called Guy Mannering and Rob Roy; and which
latter, as she intimated, some person had expanded
into a book of several volumes—for she had seen
it lying on Mrs. Lightblue's library table. "La,
Ma!"—exclaimed Juliana, somewhat impatiently,
on hearing Mrs. T. make this unexpected sally
into the confines of literature—" I'm sure we told
you no such thing. And how you do confuse
things together!—Why Guy Mannering is an
opera, written by Mr. Bishop; and it was Mr.
Terry, the actor, who wrote Rob Roy, and Sir
Walter himself who afterwards made it into a
novel."—" Well, my love"—said Mrs. T.—" you
know I don't pretend to understand so much about
these things as you do. But what was that"—she

continued—for she likes to display her daughter's
knowledge, even at the expense of her own—
"what was that you were telling me, about Sir
Walter Scott being known among his friends by
the title of *the great unknown*? What do they
mean by calling him the Great Unknown? I
thought he was better known than body, except
'the author of Waverly,' and the court of Aldermen."—"Dear me, Ma!"—said Frances—"why
you're at your confusions again—'the author of
Waverly' died long before we were born. Why
Waverly was written 'sixty years ago,' It says
so in the title-page."

Luckily the noise of knives and forks, and the
clearing of the table, prevented this enlightened
colloquy from extending beyond the immediate
precincts in which it was uttered, and where the
subjects of it were not sufficiently interesting to
render its little errors of any importance; and by
the time the desert and wine were placed on the
table, all thoughts of it had passed away, and
given place to a discussion which now arose, relative to the progress of the fine arts in this country;
in which discussion all the party seemed fully
qualified and prepared to take their share. The
point in question was, the comparative merits of
that year's Exhibition at Somerset House, (then

open,) and the previous year's;—the point having been started in consequence of some remark on the merits of a whole length likeness of Mr. Tibbs the elder, which had been recognised that very morning by two of the party, notwithstanding its modest alias of " portrait of a gentleman." On this question, as to the aforesaid progress of the fine arts generally, it is singular that every one of the party had fully made up their minds. It is no less singular too, that the judgments were pretty equally divided; about one half being decidedly of opinion that the Exhibition this year was " much better" than that of last year, and the other half feeling equally satisfied that it was " not near so good :" both parties agreeing, however, that there were " a great many portraits ;" and that the rooms were " exceedingly warm," and the company " very mixed !"

By this time the wine had passed round two or three times; and as this proceeded in its regular course (out of which Mr. T. never permits it to swerve on any consideration whatever) most of the various topics of the day came by turn into discussion ; and we may venture to say that not one of them was treated with a less conspicuous share of acumen and discrimination than had been displayed in regard to the above. What was said on

any of these subjects it would be obviously improper
for us to report at any length, however edifying
such a report might be. Suffice it to add, that,
after the fifth glass of wine, politics, as it always
does on similar occasions, became the sole order of
the day. Whereupon the ladies, accepting this as a
very intelligible signal that their company could
be dispensed with, retired to the drawing-room;
and each gentleman proceeded to take advantage of
the first opportunity that offered, of expressing his
own particular opinions on the prominent political
events and topics of the past week; each availing
himself, respectively, of the particular newspaper
to which he was attached, and each of course
being " decidedly of opinion" with that. As politics is a subject not to be ousted when once it
gets a fair footing at an English after-dinner table,
and as it is one with which we do not profess to
meddle, we shall now silently take our leave:
though we were perhaps bound to consider the
Dinner Party of the day as virtually at an end,
the moment the ladies left the table.

H.

LETTERS ON SHAKESPEARE.

BY PROFESSOR W———.

LETTERS ON SHAKESPEARE. *

No. 2.

ROMEO AND JULIET.

BY PROFESSOR W———.

MY DEAR FRIEND,

AFTER a long protracted silence, I again venture
to address you, on the subject of that divine
mind whose productions have so often occupied
and delighted *our* minds—not without occasionally overshadowing, and even overwhelming them,
with a sense of its wondrous and superhuman
power. And in truth, I am fain to confess my
belief, that it is the perhaps half-unconscious
presence of this sense, perpetually pressing upon
me whenever I have turned my thoughts to this
subject, which has so long deterred me from
fulfilling my promise, of communicating to you,

* Continued from Blackwood's Magazine, vol. 2. p. 512.

in something like a regular and tangible form, those views and feelings which we have so often discussed together, touching the true individual characters of Shakespeare's principal dramatic works.

It is not that I have feared to approach the footstool of this mighty being—this god among men; or that I have felt abashed in his imaginary presence: for HE too has said, in sentiment if not in words, " Let little children come unto me, and I will not turn them away." (To *you*, who know my heart, I need not disclaim, in this allusion, anything approaching to levity, or a disposition towards the undue mingling of sacred things with profane.) It is not, I say, that in entering the presence of this great representative of all the various powers of the divinely human intellect of man, I have experienced a more than ordinary sense of my own comparative nothingness, and have shrunk backward abashed at the contemplation: for it is one of the finest and most characteristical qualities of Shakespeare's mind, that, on feeling ourselves within the sphere of *its* action and influence, all egotism, whether it be of a vain-glorious and self-exalting, or of an equally vain-glorious though self-abasing nature, melts utterly away, and becomes merged and lost in an all absorbing sentiment of mingled admiration and love; an admiration, however, and a love, which have for their object nothing more, after all, than *human* attributes and qualities; and which therefore inspire us with anything rather than contempt for the form that we wear, and the mind that gives it life and motion. It is, in fact, only *a man* that we are listening to; and being *men* ourselves, we cannot chuse but listen with something like secret self-congratulations, on the possible greatness and beauty and power of our common nature.

No—if I am ever disposed to sink into an undue despondency of heart, and to let my coward thoughts fly before the conquering spirit of doubt that will sometimes beset them, I have only to make my stand within the stronghold of Shakespeare, and I feel instantly revived and reinstated and re-assured ; and the very spot that I had entered the moment before, cowering and crest-fallen, I am ready the next moment to quit, erect, stedfast, and heart-whole. No—of all those master-spirits upon whom we call, and bid them " minister to a mind diseased," *he* is the only one who does not, in the end, refer of that passion which is its nominal subject: I say its "nominal" subject; for, paradoxical as the assertion may at first seem, *love* is not the real subject of this tragedy, but only the accidental, or rather the incidental one—incidental to it, simply because it is, in an incomparably greater degree than all other passions, incidental to that state of being which *is* the essential subject of the work.

If Shakespeare had proposed to himself to illustrate and make manifest the various movements and qualities appertaining to and constituting the passion of love, would he have made it the first action of his lover to rise from the feet of one mistress, and, without a moment's pause, throw himself before another; forgetting from that time forth that the first had ever existed, much less held him in thrall? Is *this* the character of love? No:—but it *is* the character of youth, and *therefore* Shakespeare has made his youthful man exhibit it: for Romeo is not *a lover*, nor any other individual modification of the human character; he has, in fact, no individual and determinate *character* at all, but is a general specimen of MAN—a pure abstraction of our human nature—at that particular

period of its being which occurs exactly between boyhood and maturity, and which we call, by way of distinction, the period of *Youth*.

Is it a characteristic of love—I mean of that profound *mental* passion of which I am now speaking—to start into life in an instant, at the mere lightning glance of beauty, and to reach its full and perfect maturity even in the very hour of its birth? Oh, no!—but it *is* the characteristic of that *other* love, which constitutes so great and absorbing a portion of the " beings end and aim" of Youth.

I am confident, my dear friend, that you will not mistake me, in what I am now saying. You will not suspect me of wishing—nay, of daring —to breathe the slightest suspicion of impurity over the enchanting passion and persons of the lovers in this drama, or to throw a doubt upon the right of that passion to be called love. It was a love " pure as the *thought* of purity "— pure as is that purely intellectual love of which I have just spoken, and which cannot co-exist with *im*purity. It was *as pure as that;* but it was *not* that.

It is not my purpose to institute a comparative estimate of these two different kinds of love, but only to mark the distinction which exists be-

tween them.   And in order to this, let me say
that they differ, as everything must differ, the
sources of which are not the same.   They differ,
as the earth differs from the heavens—or rather
as their productions differ ; for one of these passions is the production of the heavenly within us,
and the other of the earthly.   But the latter is
equally pure with the former, when it exists in
the state in which they possessed it whose history
we are examining ; and it differs from its relative
only as the flowers differ from the stars, or as physical beauty differs from intellectual.   Is the rose
impure because its roots are in the earth, and its
nourishment springs from thence ? Neither then
is the love of Romeo and Juliet impure because its
roots and its food are in the flesh, not in the
spirit.

But let us look a little more closely into the
characteristic qualities of this most enchanting
of all dramas—most enchanting to all of us, because it offers, to those who are still the happy
denizens of that state of being which it represents,
an echo of the rich music that is for ever ring-
ing in their hearts ; and to those who have passed
through that state, it recalls and revives and re-
creates all that sanctified and made it sweet.

At the opening of the play, we find the hero of

it as deeply in love (as the phrase is) as words,
even the words of Shakespeare, can describe him
to be.   He is altogether a creature of passion ;
floating this way and that on the waves of it ;
blown hither and thither by its winds ; now borne
downwards into its darkest depths, and now rapt
upward to it highest and brightest heavens ; one
moment revelling in its richest fields of hope and
happiness, and the next bound hand and foot in
the dungeons of its despair.

Let it be observed, too, that we hear of all this
passion, long before we hear of its object ; and
the reader who comes to the perusal of Romeo and
Juliet for the first time, imagines, of course, that
it is Juliet who inspires it all ; or rather, he does not
tax his imagination on the subject, or ever think
of inquiring, but takes it for granted.   And I am
inclined to fear, too, that when he first comes to
discover that all these transports are felt for another, and *not* for Juliet, he is at least disappointed, if not displeased or indignant.

And yet the above is, beyond comparison, that
point in the character which shows its creator in
the most extraordinary light—which most clearly
evinces the subtlety of his conceptions, and his
astonishing boldness in developing them.   No
poet that ever lived, except Shakespeare, would

have thought of proving the depth and sincerity
of his hero's love for his *present* mistress, by representing him as feeling and expressing it for the
first time, in the very presence of her who *was* his
mistress half an hour ago, and for whom he would
then have professed and acted all that he *now* will
for his new one. And yet, instead of feeling that
Romeo's late professions of love for Rosaline throw
any suspicion upon the sincerity of his present
love for Juliet, there can be no doubt whatever
that the effect is exactly the reverse. I say the
effect ; for I believe that those (even among female
readers) who make it a question with themselves
whether this fickleness, as they would call it, does
or does not affect the value of Romeo's later
passion, are at first inclined to determine, that at
any rate Rosaline had his *first* love. But let a
Romeo of real life transfer his transports from another to *them ;* and at the same time, let another
adorer of equal pretensions, lay at their feet the
prémices of his heart ; and see whether they will
not incline to the first rather than the second.
And this, not from any feeling of gratified vanity
at the *preference*, but from an instinctive sense of
the spontaneous nature of the love of youth, and
its consequent incapacity of waiting for a particu
lar object before it becomes developed. Every

woman believes, and is bound to believe, that *she* is the only object that could have *fixed* her lover. But she does not think him the less fixed because his love was lent to another before it was given to her; nor does she covet it the less because she cannot look upon herself as its creator. It is for man, not woman, to cherish a feeling so nearly allied to selfishness.

But another effect of representing Romeo as experienced in the ways of love, long before he meets with the true object of it, is, to aggrandise our sense of the power and weight of his passion, when it comes to be transferred to its ultimate destination. It was absolutely necessary to the conduct of the story, that we should see the *commencement* of the love of Romeo for Juliet. And it was equally necessary that we should attach a certain value and importance to that love. But we have no great faith in either the force or the stability of a passion which is conceived and born before our eyes. Accordingly, Romeo is placed before us, the very concentration or personification of passion. " Passion !" Mercutio calls him ; as if it were his name. He is all made up of it. And when he sees what we all along feel to be the legitimate object of that passion, he has nothing to do but pour it all out into her heart, and disburthen himself of what has hitherto been pressing upon him with a weight " heavy as frost, and deep almost as life ;" but heavy and oppressive only because it could not find the object that was destined to receive and share it : as the clouds go heavily and darkly along, while they are surcharged with the bright rain, but become bright and bouyant themselves the moment they come near enough to the earth to part with their fertilizing burthen.

If Romeo's love had been the love of a moment, we should never have endured the train of consequences that flow from it, but should have regarded them in the anomalous light of effects without an adequate cause. But as it is, that weight of passion (the accumulation of years perhaps) which he pours forth at once into the heart of Juliet the moment he beholds her, is cause enough for any effect that can flow from it.

I will not scruple to confess, that the good effect which is produced by Romeo presenting himself before Juliet with a heart already filled to overflowing with passion, is not gained without some counterbalancing evil. And if Rosaline, the first object of that passion, had been brought forward in the play, in a visible form, this evil would have been still more manifest. But, to say nothing of her not returning his passion, she is but *a name* in our imagination, after all——not a person. And, to shew how entirely Shakespeare has gained his object in making Rosaline *only* a name, it is but necessary to appeal to every ordinary reader and spectator of the play, who, on referring to their feelings on the point in question, will find that they scarcely remember that such a person is alluded to.

If, indeed, Rosaline had been represented to us as the accepting and accepted mistress of Romeo, and his change of allegiance had come upon us in the light of a *desertion*, the case would have been widely different, and its effect on the whole after part of the drama would have been mischievous, and indeed intolerable.

But why, you ask, contemplate a case which was never contemplated by Shakespeare? I accept the reproof, and at once return to him and his divine work;——for I shall have quite enough to do to explain to you my views of what this play *is*, without speculating on what it *might have been*.

The love of Romeo and Juliet must be regarded, then, as the manifestation of that passion (call it by what name you will) which is the dominating spirit of that period of human life of which these lovers are the type and representa-

tive ;—a period when to live and to love are one,
and the life of which and its love expire together ;
as we see mystically shadowed forth in the deaths
of these two beings. It has every characteristic
of that period : its headlong precipitancy ; its
heedless rashness ; its total disregard of all
worldly considerations or consequences ; its enthusiastic ardour of aspiration, and force of will ;
its unhesitating confidence in the reality of all
which does but seem, whether of good or of
evil ; its proness to seize, without an instant's
delay, on all that the hand of pleasure proffers,
without asking the price, or calculating the comparative value ; and above all, that boundless capacity for enjoyment and for suffering, which one
moment lifts it to the highest empyrean of bliss,
and the next sinks it to the lowest dungeons of
despair.

So true does it seem, to me that Romeo and
Juliet are mere abstractions, or rather that the
two are *an* abstraction of human life at a particular period of it ; or, perhaps it were better to
say, of the human being in its dual state, of
man and woman; that if we examine our feelings in regard to their *characters*, (as we are accustomed to phrase it,) we shall find that we do
not recognize anything in the shape of indivi-

duality, or of intellectual portraiture, in either of them : which I will venture to say is not the case with any one other of the creations of Shakespeare's hand.

Neither do we connect with the lovers any imaginary association whatever, appertaining to external form : which truth, if it be one, is equally with the above confined to them alone.

If we were to descend from this general statement of the proposition, and examine every separate sentiment or sentence uttered by each of them throughout the play, it would probably lead to the same conclusion. And the reason is, that they utter, not the results of that complicated condition of being which we call *character*, and which consists of a thousand modifying influences and impulses ; but of passion—passion, which is one and indivisible, and which is the same yesterday, to-day, and for ever ;—passion, which circumstances may repress, or keep out of sight, or even destroy ; but which nothing can *change :* which is in fact not susceptible of change, in the very nature of things ; because it is in our passions that our *human being* consists ; and while *that* remains, they must remain too ; and while *they* remain, their result must be universally and unchangeably the same.

Such, my dear friend, are the conceptions which I have formed of the two principal persons of this divinely human work. Let me not quit them, however, without following them to their fragrant grave, and seeing them quietly inurned there : for, untimely as that grave is, it is still sweet, since each finds it in the arms of the other, and exhales over it the sweetest sighs that were ever breathed from the lips of loveliness.

Let me approach it, too, without a thought of sorrow, nor shed over it one profaning tear ; for they whom it encloses shed none, but laid themselves down in it as if it had been their bridal bed : which in truth it was ; for they had no other.

No—let us utter no idle lamentations over the early death of these lovers, either on their account, or our own ; for had they lived they would have ceased to *be* lovers, both for us and for themselves. If the flowers were not to die almost in the hour of their birth, they would be born in vain ; and if the state of being which these lovers typify were not as fleeting as it is fair, its fairness would be forgotten or disregarded long before it was passed away.

Doubtless Shakespeare intended that this should be the condition of our feelings in regard to the deaths of Romeo and Juliet; for he has inflicted no positive pain upon them, either physical or intellectual; no " longing, lingering looks" are cast behind them as they pass away from our sight; but all is anticipation and hope; each being dead to the other, and each therefore hastening to join its other self. It is to each as if its soul had passed away beforehand, and there was nothing left for the deserted body to do, but melt meekly into the bosom of its parent earth, and mingle with the elements from whence it arose.

The catastrophe of Romeo and Juliet is expressly contrived with a view to this avoidance of all painful impressions at our parting with this pair of " star-crossed lovers ;" and no other arrangement but that which has been adopted could have accomplished this view. As for Juliet,— " the weaker vessel "—she is put gently to sleep the moment that adverse circumstances are at hand ; and she only awakes to see her lord lying at her feet, and to pour forth her soul into his still warm bosom. While he, having been struck dead at once, in spirit, by the account of *her* death, has nothing to do, and never for an instant even *thinks* of doing anything, but seek himself out " a triumphant grave," and pass into it, drinking an almost jocund health to his love : for

K

that he feels to be immortal, even at the very moment when its object lies dead before his eyes.

Let it be observed, too, that none of the ordinary concomitants of death are admitted into this closing scene of the lives of our lovers. As for Juliet,—her beauty is upon her, bright as ever. And though, from the supposed truth of his information as to her death, Romeo *believes* her to be dead, yet he evidently *feels* that she is *not* dead, and dies himself in the half-voluptuous kiss that recals her to life.

<blockquote>
"Here's to my love!"   *   *   *   *

*   *   *   "Thus with a kiss I die!"
</blockquote>

While she, so recalled to life, does but ask for her husband; and at once finding him, and finding him not, replies to his kiss by another, (the *first* and the *last* of each) and so dies too, with the "*warm*" pressure of his lips upon hers.

<blockquote>
"Thy lips are warm!"
</blockquote>

What is there of death here? what of the grave? It is but the spirit of youth, exhaling itself away in sweet sighs, to the music of meeting lips. And if you would not think me too fanciful, I would add,—with reference to what I have before hinted, as to the nature of Romeo and Juliet's love,—that this scene is, perchance, merely intended to be typical of the natural and necessary death of that particular species of love which cannot survive fruition even for a moment, at least under its original form and character; but, when it does survive it, assumes a new form, and rises into that intellectual love which is immortal as the soul that is its seat. Each of the lovers seeks death—each dies willingly, and without a reverting look—and each expires instantly on pressing its lips to those of the other. And we may, if we please, fancy that each presently arises from its " triumphant grave," in another and a better world ; assoiled from all its earthly weaknesses and woes, and living, and to live for ever.

Perhaps I ought to apologize, even to you, for dwelling so long on this particular point in the drama, and still more for dwelling on it in terms which I fear you will at least not admire for their sobriety. But the truth is, I never can keep my feelings, in regard to this part of the drama, (and therefore not my expressions), within very strict bounds, when I think upon the base and senseless profanation which has been practised on it by some ignorant modern hand, and universally adopted by the still more ignorant players in their

K 2

representation of it.   The catastrophe was not *tragic* enough, forsooth ; and they must have the lovers meet face to face, and die in each others arms by lingering torments : the one torn to pieces in body by the physical effects of the poison, and in mind by the still more terrible poison of rage and despair at seeing his lady living after he has killed himself to be with her ; and the other, racked and riven still more fearfully at the sight of all these horrors,—till she has scarcely strength left in her tender body and exhausted mind, to let out that life which it would be madness to keep a moment longer, after witnessing the scene which *they* make her witness !

But let us not be too angry with those who knew not what they did, and whose crime included its own punishment.   We need not wish them worse than to want that which, having, they could not have perpetrated the profanation of which I speak.   Though it is scarcely just to indulge towards them any feeling approaching to pity and forgiveness, when we recollect how many thousands of their betters they have deprived of that delight which they will now never experience, of witnessing the true and natural catastrophe of this drama, and of enjoying it as their natural sense of the true and beautiful would have led them to do : for there can be little doubt that, even in this age of readers, scarcely one person in a thousand knows any thing of Shakespeare, but what they have seen on the stage.

Let us now return to a more general consideration of this divine drama. It is not in the two principal persons alone that that spirit of youth prevails, which I have spoken of as the predominating character of the work. All are alike embued with it ; it renders all buoyant and full of life ; it is an abiding presence which pervades and interpenetrates all, and in so doing creates that dramatic unity of effect which is so indispensable to the highest species of drama, and which is so rarely to be met with out of Shakespeare.

A glance at the principal secondary characters will make manifest the truth of what I am stating. What is old Capulet, but a grey-headed youth ? Age has had its inevitable effect upon his body, it is true ; for physical things cannot resist it. But his mind has escaped its power, and is as young as when he was a hair-brained school-boy. He is as eager and hot-hearted in the pursuit of an imaginary quarrel, as he was then ; as delighted at the anticipation of a feast and revelry, and as animated and light-hearted when it arrives ; as precipitate in making up his mind on points of vital importance, and as headstrong in maintaining his hasty determinations; as free and generous in his expenditure ; as happy at the sight of others happiness ;—in short, he has no one quality of age, but that one which half-translates age into youth, by recalling and recreating all that it then felt, and thought, and acted : I mean its gay-hearted garrulousness.   An old man who is perpetually talking over the exploits of his youth, and finds no lack of listeners, is happier than when he was acting them ; and, in effect, he is younger; for he has already reached that period the anticipation of which is the only curse of youth : he is young, without the fear before him of growing old.

The rest of the old people are scarcely less happily gifted than Capulet.   Even Friar Lawrence is no exception.   However he may deceive himself and others by having wise proverbs on his lips, his heart is as young as a romantic school-girl's ; and he does not hesitate for a single instant (any more than she would) to assist his young friend and pupil in committing an insane marriage with the daughter of his direst foe.

"Wisely and slow ; they stumble that run fast;" he *says*. And then he goes immediately and marries a couple, whose acquaintance is the growth of half an hour !

He is a poet, too.   Not a word he utters but what is steeped in the rich music of the imagination.   And poets are ever young.   Hark how he greets the first approach of the lady Juliet to his lonely cell.   It is the very spirit of youth and of poetry combined, that speaks :

> " Here comes the lady.   O, so light a foot
> Will ne'er wear out the everlasting flints.
> A lover may bestride the gossamers
> That idle in the wanton summer air,
> And yet not fall : so light is vanity !"

And as for the delightful old Nurse—she is the youngest of all the party.   Her tongue seems to have the power as well as the privilege of childhood ; and whether it has anything or nothing to say, runs babbling on like a summer brook.

But if the old people are all young, what shall we say of the young ones ? of Mercutio, Tybalt, County Paris, and the rest ?—What—but that they are all more or less embued with the prevailing spirit of the drama ; and that in none of them is that spirit blended with any *other ;*—and that the first named—Mercutio—is the very quintessential extract—the *spirit* of that spirit.   He is as young as the rest of his companions, without like them having yet tasted of that bitter-sweet fruit of youth which is the first step towards age.   He is like them in all other respects ; but with this (to him at least) manifest advantage over them—that he can jest all day long at that which is the only serious thing in the world to them.   And even when death comes upon him in the midst of his mad-brained joy, he will not yield to the summons, but struggles jestingly against it ; as if it were nothing more than an impertinent creditor arresting him on his way to a feast.

There is still one other person of this drama, whom you must not suppose that I have forgotten; still less must you imagine that I would intentionally overlook him, from any feeling that his introduction militates against that *unity* of effect which, I have said, is so finely spread over the whole design, and wrought into the whole texture, of this perfect work.   I mean the Apothecary. So far from wishing to do so, I conceive that he is no less essential to the due bringing-out of the effect (to use a painter's phrase), than any one other person in the drama.   And this alone is a sufficient reason for finding him here.

But even putting aside this view of the matter,— if it were not for him, the impression received from the whole work would be too buoyant, and full of the spirit of youth, to be a true echo of any impression which we *can* receive from the contemplation of any actual portion of our human life : which imitative impression is what every one of Shakespeare's dramas is intended to create, and in fact does create.

The two extremes of our existence—Life and Death—like all other extremes, meet. They are necessary corollaries from each other ; and we can no more contemplate one absent from the other, than we can the two extremes of a continuous line. Now, the idea of the Apothecary perpetually haunts our imagination when we are thinking of the play of Romeo and Juliet, just as the idea of Death haunts it when we are thinking even of the brightest and freshest portions of our Human Life. And the idea just as little *disturbs* the general impressions we receive in either case. It does not disturb, but only modifies them, by blending them with others, which, in taking away a little of their brightness, add to rather than diminish their moral beauty. The idea, in both cases, serves but as a gentle *memento mori*,— endearing the objects and images with which it blends ; even as I have seen it do in the burial-places of a foreign land, when engraven on a

little cross of black wood, planted on an infant's
grave, and almost hidden among the bright flowers
that garland and grow around it.

Permit me, my dear friend, before closing this
inordinately long letter, to warn you (though I feel
assured that the warning is superfluous) against
judging of what I have now said of this sweetest,
gentlest, and most perfect of all Shakespeare's
productions, in the presence of any of those impressions which you may have received from
witnessing the *acted* play. And this warning is
particularly necessary (if at all) in connection with
the latter part of my remarks. I have there supposed that this drama *requires* some one idea or
image, to balance that exuberant spirit of life
which everywhere pervades it; and that, therefore, Shakespeare has introduced the one alluded
to. Need I add, then, that I speak of *Shakespeare's* drama, *not* of that which has been polluted
by the impudent interpolations of the players?
Heaven knows, the general impression left by the
catastrophe of this latter, when represented, as we
have seen it, by consummate actors, is enough to
embitter a whole after life, and half blight the recollections of the past, however bright they may
have been! Assuredly, *that* is enough to coun-
terbalance a thousand fold all the buoyancy that

has gone before it, even though the " overwhelming brows," and haggard, and famine stricken
visage of the poor Apothecary, were to be transformed, by the same kind of play-house magic,
into the sparkling eyes and rubicund cheeks of
some fat and contented Friar: which transformation, by the bye, would be quite as natural and
necessary to the consistency of the work.

No—never did I see an essential change made
in any of Shakespeare's dramas, that was not infinitely for the worse; and *this* is infinitely the
worst of all. So that you will not wonder if I
am a little anxious that you should not inadver-
tently try anything I have said of Romeo and
Juliet, by the impressions received from this version of it—which absolutely destroys the very
essence of its character, and changes it, so far as
regards the catastrophe, from a perfect drama of
the very highest class, into a paltry *melo*-drama, of
the very lowest.

It was my intention to have said something on
the *poetry* of this divine production, both as distinguished from, and as blended with, its passion;
and also of the exquisite language in which both
are conveyed. But I must reserve these remarks
for another letter. Your affectionate friend,

T. C.

GRIMM'S GHOST.

THE CULPEPPERS ON THE CONTINENT.

BY THE OTHER OF THE AUTHORS OF " REJECTED ADDRESSES."

GRIMM'S GHOST.*

THE CULPEPPERS ON THE CONTINENT.

BY THE OTHER OF THE AUTHORS OF " REJECTED ADDRESSES."

THE Culpeppers and the Dixons have made numerous and noticeable advances in the ways of *haut ton,* since I last had occasion to report progress on their proceedings. It is true they still " hang out," (as Ned Culpepper in his less refined moments phrases it), in Savage Gardens, —seeing that the leases of their respective residences have yet some years to run, and neither party has hitherto hit upon any effectual method of quickening the pace of those parchment ponies. But in default of being able to remove their domiciles to the desiderated purlieus of the Regent's Park, they have done what they justly deem the next best thing, in transferring, as much as may be, the air of the said Park to

* See New Monthly Magazine *passim*.

Savage Gardens.   Not being at present in a condition to go to the mountain, they have contrived to make the mountain come to them.   In short, by the aid of Mr. Parker's patent cosmetic for the cure of cracks in the complexions of decaying walls, (which, by the bye, like all other cosmetics, requires to be " laid on with a trowel"), they have struck off a century from the seeming age of their now " modern antique" dwellings, and made them as pretty illustrations as need be of " the Deformed Transformed."

Both parties, too, were determined " not to stick at trifles," as Ned reports, " but do the thing handsome while they were about it."   And accordingly, this memorable change has been effected no less *intus* than *in cute;* and now, Captain Augustus Thackery would no more recognise the dark, dingy drawing-room, with its grey wainscotted walls, in which I have recorded his first hospitable reception by the Culpeppers, than he did his own face in the glass the other day, after having permitted it to be so pitilessly mulct of the major part of its mustachios.

The said drawing-room has been forced, by the friendly intervention of a pair of folding doors, into a fashionable alliance with its late neighbour the back bed-room adjoining, and the latter has of course assumed the name and arms of the former ; while the windows of each have been duly cut down to the floor and raised up to the ceiling, according to the newest mode in that case made and provided for letting in the cold ; and the antique mouldings of the wainscot have been macadamized into a smooth plain of French *tapisserie,* on which the whole heathen mythology are manifesting themselves under the most amiable attitudes.

The furniture has also undergone a no less radical reform. The grim old Kidderminster is discarded in favour of a brilliant Brussels of a kaleidoscope pattern. The eight huge, stiff-legged and high-shouldered arm-chairs, each as big as a sofa-bedstead, have been changed for a dozen of trim little rose-wood receptacles, with legs as crooked as ram's horns, and backs that laugh lolling to scorn ; besides a tastily-turned Grecian couch to match,—constructed (for the convenience of modern Routers) on the express principle of preventing people from going to sleep : —to say nothing of a *settee* in each window, the like of which, as Old Culpepper facetiously observes, was never seen in the *Cittee* before.

As for the rest of the furniture, it has undergone an entire " French Revolution." There is a French *Console* in the pier; (" *Consols* are deuced high!" said old C. when he saw the bill of it); a French clock and French china on the mantle-piece; a French glass over the fire-place; French lamps on the French-fashioned card-tables; and French polish on everything in the room, except its inhabitants.

Perhaps it was an amiably unconscious consciousness of this last-named deficiency, which prompted the similar and simultaneous proposal of Mrs. Culpepper and Mrs. Dixon to their respective, respected, and respectable spouses, the results of which I am now to report : premising, however, that, whatever the censorious may insinuate to the contrary, the almost identical periods and idioms at and in which these two proposals were promulgated, do not by any means demonstrate a previous concert on the part of these prudent consorts, touching the point in question. Not that I take upon me to deny, any more than to asseverate, said concert between said consorts. I leave the point to be settled between the future commentators on these immortal epistles.

" Railly, $\left\{ \begin{array}{c} \text{Dixon,} \\ \text{Culpepper,} \end{array} \right\}$ " said Mrs. $\left\{ \begin{array}{c} \text{D.} \\ \text{C.} \end{array} \right\}$ as the family quartett sat looking at each other just after dinner, opposite the four points of the

flowery compass impressed in centre of the
newly calendered blue baize cover of the cushion-
shaped dining-table—" Railly, { Dixon Culpepper } I
think the young people ought to see some'at of
foreign parts now. Not but what Margate is
monstrous genteel, and frequented by the rail tip-
toppers of Trinity Square and the Crescent—
especially since the steamers have run so regular and cheap. But then, you know, one
does'nt see any of the continent at Margate—
and I'm sure it must be a fine sight, from what
Captain Thackery said about it the other day—
though I cou'dn't very well make out what it was
like. I'm told, too, it's to be seen just as well
at Bullen as if you went all the way to Jamaica
to look at it. Now what do you say, my love, to
taking us all over for a week or ten days? I've
heard it's only like crossing over the way, in a
manner speaking. Now I think of it, too, I
shou'dn't wonder a bit if our next door neighbours
would like to jine us—and that would make it
come quite easy, you know—for then we could
all be together, and have our meals under one.
Besides,—I railly do think the young folks ought
to see some'at of foreign ways. Why there's

them Hincks's gals have been to Rome, and Italy, and the Rhine, and"——

The elder Culpepper's patience, which was generally quite exemplary under the infliction of an apparently interminable harangue of this nature, would probably have stood him in stead some time longer. But his love of a joke (provided he himself was the ostensible projector of it) was not so easily to be kept under; and accordingly, this mention of the Rhine roused him from his chin-on-elbow-supported attitude, in a moment.

" The *Rind!*" reiterated he with a good-humoured chuckle—" ha ! ha ! the Rind ! they need'nt go far to see that. They've only to step into our friend Dixon's shop in Fenchurch Street, and they may see plenty of the *Rind,* and smell it too, for that matter."*

There are certain kinds of puns the mere odour of which, like that of " the morning air" to the ghost of Hamlet's father, is potent enough to drive a disembodied spirit like myself out of the room in which they are engendered. And

---

* I hope I need not recall to the reader's recollection that Mr. Andrew Dixon is the senior partner in an eminent cheesemongering concern in Fenchurch-street.

this of Old Culpepper's was one of them. I am therefore not able to report by what more cogent arguments than those urged above, the ladies respectively of Messrs. Culpepper and Dixon prevailed upon their lords not only to allow of, but partake in, the projected excursion to " Bullen." But that they *did* so prevail will scarcely be considered as problematical, when I aver that the Friday following saw the whole party of eight duly installed on the deck of the Superb, steaming away down the river, to their hearts' content.

Having, in my present state of being, a mortal or rather an *im*mortal antipathy to anything in the shape of smoke, the reader will not be surprised to learn that I declined accompanying our travellers any farther than to see them safe off from the Tower stairs. I must therefore consign to another pen the task of communicating the events consequent on the voyage.

MISS CLARA CULPEPPER TO HER FRIEND MISS BELINA BINKS OF BUCKLERSBURY.

Boulogne, Friday Evening, Sept. 1825.

Well, my love! here we are in France, sure enough! but after *such* a voyage!—oh my dear, the ocean is a frightful beast to be tossed about upon the back of, I do assure you. It was all very well at first. Just for all the world like going to Margate, only the company was far genteeler. But after we had made as nice a little pic-nic dinner as could be, off the contents of our hamper, and were just thinking of having a comfortable cup of tea—oh, my dear! the wind began to blow—(a " breeze," they called it—a pretty *breeze* it kicked up among all of us, sure enough!)—the sea began to swell up every here and there, just as it does in the last scene of Paul and Virginia, only worse if anything— and all in a moment I began to be *so* sick, and *so* frightened, and Pa was *so* cross about having consented to come, and Ma was *so* angry with Ned and me for having persuaded her to persuade him, and Ned, (who did'nt seem to mind it a bit,) was *so* provoking, and everything was *so* disagreeable, that I can't bear even to think of it now it's all over; so I shall only say that the nasty sea water has quite annihilated my sweet green spencer, and turned Ma's crimson pelisse all over as black as the chimney, and run away with Pa's hat, and what's most provoking of all, has got into the box that held all Ma's and my pretty lisse caps and frills, and washed them all up into a little dirty bundle in one corner.

This is all I can tell you to-night, my love; for Ma is *so* cross about the caps and frills that she says I sha'nt sit up a minute longer. But to-morrow I mean to take up my pen again, and then I've got *such* things to tell you! Oh, my dear Bel, you can't imagine what very odd things happened to us when we first got here. But Ma won't let me scribble, as she calls it, any longer —so good night.

Saturday Morning.

Well, my love—I feel quite recovered from the fatigues and disasters of yesterday—and I expect to pass the charmingest day, and I'm *so* delighted with France—at least I think I shall be —and—but I must tell you about our landing first, for I don't think we shall meet with anything so odd as that, if we stay here till Christmas.

When we got opposite the Porte of Boulogne— (I'm sorry to say I can't tell you anything that happened till then, I was so shocking ill)—but when we got to the Porte—(By the bye, I wonder, my dear, what they can mean by calling it the *Porte* of Boulogne. *Porte*, you know, means *door*, in French—and there's not a bit of a door, or anything of the sort—it all lays as open as Blackheath—but, now I think of it, captains of ships, and such kind of persons, can't be expected to understand French)—however, when, as I was saying, we got opposite Boulogne, what do you think the odious captain did? He made a dead stop at about a quarter of a mile from the town, and pretended he could'nt get in—that there was'nt room, or water enough, or some such nonsensical excuse! Why, he must have thought us all fools, I suppose, or blind—for there was oceans of water—you could hardly see anything else—and as for room, there was enough for fifty ships as big as his to have gone in side by side. Ned said it was " a regular take in"—but Pa said he did'nt see how it could be a " take in"—that if they would but *take us in*, it was all we wanted—but as far as he could see they seemed determined on keeping us out. However, when they found that we would not get out into the nasty little ships that came from the town to fetch us, and that looked, as Mr. Dixon said, like great empty butter casks cut down the middle, and a scaffold pole stuck up in them with a dirty sheet tied to it,—they at last took us into the harbour.

By the bye, calling this place the *harbour* was the first thing that set Ma off about the inferiorness of the French to us. She said if they

did'nt know what a *harbour* was, better than that,
it was a pity somebody did'nt learn them—for
it was no more like the one in which she had so
often took tea at the bottom of Mr. Mince's
garden in Camberwell Grove, than nothing at all.

By this time you must suppose us got close
up to the side of the water, just as it might be
at Billingsgate, only nothing like it at all, but
quite different. Here we were met by a string
of people who had been following by the side of
us for ever so far, and making such frightful and
outlandish noises that I was actually afraid to
look up and see what it was all about. But
when we stopped close to the side, and I *did* look
up—la! my love, it was really quite shocking, I
do assure you, besides its being by no means
what Ma calls *proper*. Do you know there was
I dare say a dozen *women*, some dragging at the
ropes that were tied to our ship, and others
squabbling and squalling at each other, about who
should be the first to lift into the ship a huge
staircase, on which we were to climb up. And
all this while there was a whole lot of big sailor-
looking men, lolling about doing nothing, and never
offering to help them !

But this was nothing, my love, to the state of
these poor women's dress, or rather their undress.

Do you know they had on neither bonnets, nor gowns, nor—in short, my dear, they did not seem to me to have anything on but their stays and under petticoats—and *they* actually reached up to their knees! I declare I did not not know what to do, or which way to look, especially when I saw Ned and George Dixon whispering and smiling to each other, and then casting impudent leers at Miss Dixon and me.

It was night, to be sure, though it was quite a fine moonlight. If it had been in the day time I'm sure I don't know what I *should* have done. Though, I've been thinking since, that the reason of this very unpleasant circumstance was, that the poor creatures, not expecting our arrival, had gone to bed, and were called up in such a hurry that they had not time to put their things on.

Well—after a deal of fuss and to do, we landed at last; and when we had got ourselves all together, two and two, under the directions of Pa, and were going to march off towards the Inn which had been recommended to us by a very polite French gentleman in the crowd, as " dee onlee good for genteelfolks," and he was even so kind as to offer to shew us the way to it himself, which Pa said was doing the civil thing in a way he did'nt expect to meet with in a foreign country—I say, just as we were going to set off, what do you think ? We found that some French fellows, with great cocked hats like the lord mayor's footmen, and great swords by their sides, had actually drawn an enormous chain all round us, to prevent our getting away—and they would'nt let a soul of us pass !

La ! my love, you can't think how frightened I was—though I did'nt say anything. And as for Ma—she was ready to drop. And well she might, for she told us afterwards she thought that a war had broke out between us and the French since the morning, and that they had let us come into their nasty town on purpose to make prisoners of war of all of us.

But we soon found that they only did this out of civility, to keep us together till all were landed, that we might then go the Custom House and show our tickets—for do you know Pa was obliged to make interest with a great French lord in London before we came away, to get tickets for all of us—(passports they call them in French)—or else they would not have let us in. And I think this is very proper—for you know if it was not for this *anybody* might come, and then how could one expect the company to be so select as it

is? Well—when everybody was out of the ship,
they let down a bit of the great chain that kept us
together, and away we all marched, two and two,
to the Custom House, to give in our tickets, and
then to the Inn, attended all the way by the civil
French gentleman I told you of before, who we
heard afterwards was no less a person than a Commissioner—though Pa said he could not find out
whether he was a Commissioner of the Customs,
or the Excise.

I think, by the bye, Pa might have asked him
to dinner, for he was uncommon civil and attentive, to be sure. And he spoke very good
English, too, considering he was only a Frenchman.

And now good bye, my dear Bel, for a day or
two; for I have neither time nor room to tell
you any more at present. And I'm afraid *this*
is so crossed and crossed that you will not be able
to make it out. Adieu.

                    Your devoted friend

                              C. C.

P. S. I must find a little corner to tell you
that young Dixon (Dixon's a nasty name—is'nt
it?—not half so genteel as Culpepper)—but he
has been vastly attentive. And if it was'nt for
the recollections of the handsome and interest-

ing Captain Augustus Thackery (that *is* something like a name!)—I—but I can't squeeze in a word more.

Boulogne, Saturday Evening.

OH! my dear Bel! Something *so* interesting has happened. It's quite like one of Miss What's-her-name's novels. You know I was telling you in my last letter that that foolish chap George Dixon had been pestering me with his " attentions," as he calls them ; and I told you too, or at least I should, if I had had room, how I hate and detest his awkward attempts at what Ned calls " doing the polite." I believe too that a word or two escaped me, on that one soft secret of my susceptible heart, which has been confided to your sympathetic bosom alone.

Well, my love, would you believe it ? Who should we meet here, the very first person on going out this morning to look about us in the town, but the Captain himself! But I must begin where I left off, and tell it you all regular, or else I shall never overtake myself, for you know I promised to tell you all that happened to us.

You may suppose we were all too tired and too ill on the night of our arrival, to make many very particular observations on the manners and customs of the French people. But as soon as ever I got up in the morning I determined to begin—for I've often told you how it used to provoke me to sit and hear that conceited Miss Christie, of Crutched Friars, tell a parcel of things about France, and not be able to contradict anything she said. So as soon as ever I had written my letter to you, I began to put everything ˈdown in a nice little note-book I made Pa buy me before we came away—especially as I promised him I would do everything in the world to improve my mind, if he would but bring us here. Besides—the captain is so clever and accomplished, that if—but this is not what I was going to say.

Sarah Dixon and I slept in the same room—for you know I should have been terrified out of my life to sleep in a room by myself in a foreign country. Well—about nine o'clock the Captain —no—I mean Ned knocked at our door, and bid us make haste down, for the Captain—no —I mean the breakfast was ready, and Pa was waiting—and that—la! my love—I really cannot stay to tell you all these uninteresting things, which happened just as they might have done at Margate or at home. I can tell you all these, you know, when we meet—especially as I'm sure you must be dying to know how it all happened about the Captain, and how he looks, and what he said, and every thing. So I shall merely say that we had a nice breakfast of regular English tea and eggs, dry toast, and twists, and a nice little plate of beef—just as it might have been at Dandelion—(I knew it was all stories that Miss Christie was telling, about the strangeness of the French customs, and about their eating dinners for breakfast)—and then we all went and dressed to go out.

Sarah Dixon would put on that odious frock of her's, with the great staring crimson stripe on the green ground, which you know we both agreed she looks so very vulgar in. But I did not say anything to her about it, for she will have her own way.

I'll tell you exactly how I was dressed—and I must say I thought I never looked neater. I had on a new morning frock that Pa bought me just before we came away. The sweetest thing! —*so* new, and *so* genteel, and *so* French—and made *so* pretty *à la blouse* as the French call it. I got Ma to let me have it made at the west end—in Sydney's Alley. It's the sweetest pattern you ever saw—a crimson and blue stripe shaded off somehow into nothing, just like a rainbow upon a primrose ground—and then a sort of zigzag running all over it—for all the world like thunder and lightning. It comes high up at the throat—and has five broad tucks made the cross way—and I've got the sweetest scarlet leather cincture for it, with a steel buckle to buckle on the left side. I wore nothing over it but a green silk half handkerchief buckled into the band behind and before—for you know I told you the nasty sea water annihilated all our frills, and I did'nt like to be beholden to Sarah Dixon for one —especially as her's are all so odiously ugly.

I had on my head my pretty little pink silk cottage bonnet—that one, you know, that every body says I look so nice in—that only just comes even with my face, and shews my profile—that everybody says—I mean that the Captain said yesterday—I mean—la! my dear—what *do* I mean?—How very confused I do get. I was going to say that under the bonnet I wore that sweet little lace cap that I bought that morning at the Bazaar when you were with me—don't you remember? And under that I wore the sweetest pair of rose-buds stuck one just over each temple. And then, you know, all my nice corkskrew curls that I had kept in papers for two whole days on purpose. You know every body says what nice hair I have, and how nice

I do it—and as for the Captain—*he* says—but stay
—I'm not come to him yet.

Well, my dear, I've now told you exactly how
I was dressed, except that I had on my nankeen
boots which lace up inside, and fit me so delight-
fully that I can hardly walk in them. As for Pa
and Ma, and old Mr. and Mrs. Dixon, I can't
stay to tell you how *they* were dressed, except
that Pa will keep wearing those nasty gaiters
that he bought in Cranbourne Alley, and that I
believe he wears on purpose that he may have to
tell everybody they are *alley gaiters**—though
why they laugh when he tells them so, I never
could make out, or why, if it's such a laughing
matter, he should be so fond of telling it.

But la ! my dear—I shall fill my paper again,
without getting to the dear Captain. As I was
saying, we all got ready to go out immediately
after breakfast, and at last out we sallied, two
and two in a string—Pa and Ma and Mr. and
Mrs. Dixon walking together by themselves, and
we young ones following—though Ned would
not walk with me as I wanted him, but would
make me take hold of that foolish George Dixon's
arm, though he knows very well how I hate him,
and how provoked I should be if the Captain—I

* Qy. *alligators.*—*Printer's Devil..*

M

mean how provoked I was when the Captain—in
short, my dear, we had hardly walked half the
length of the street in which the inn is, and were
all standing still in a row looking up at the beauti-
fullest picture you ever saw, which is oddly enough
stuck up outside the house instead of inside, and
which Pa says he asked a gentleman that he met
at the inn since, how it came to be hung *outside*
the house, and what it was a picture of—and the
gentleman said it was a sign—and Pa said a sign
of what? and the gentleman smiled, and said it
was a sign that the French artists are the best sign
painters in the world, and—but where was I—
oh—we were all standing still, looking up at this
beautiful picture—when who should I see pass by
us but Captain Augustus Thackery himself! I
knew him in a moment—though he has had almost
all his beautiful whiskers cut off, and had on
only a common blue coat, and white pantaloons,
and did'nt look like a captain at all.

La! my dear, you might have knocked me
down with a feather. My heart did beat so,
you can't think. Meeting him, you know, under
such very romantic circumstances—in a foreign
country—and so unexpectedly—and I hold of that
nasty George Dixon's arm too—and every thing.

I declare I did'nt know what to do. However, I had plenty of time to recover myself—for though the Captain looked full at us all as he passed—at least at me and Sarah Dixon—and turned round to look at us after he got by—yet he did'nt know us a bit, no more than if he had never seen us. I think I told you he wears a beautiful quizzing glass—which accounts for his not seeing us. Well—on he passed without ever seeing us, though he looked at us all the time. And to tell you the truth, I'm not sorry for it now—though I was monstrously disappointed at the time—for if he *had* seen us, and come up and spoke to us, I declare I do think I should have dropped. You see, my dear Bel, I have filled my paper cram full again, without getting to the end—or rather hardly to the beginning—of our adventure with the Captain. But to-morrow I mean to devote a whole sheet to nothing else—about how we met him again the same evening when I was walking alone with George Dixon—and how he *did* see us then the moment he came near us—and how he came up to me and took hold of my hand—and how—in short, every thing about it. So adieu till to-morrow dear Bel.

Ever your devoted friend,

C. C.

THE SPIRIT OF THE AGE.

WILLIAM HAZLITT.

THE SPIRIT OF THE AGE. *

WILLIAM HAZLITT.

We are going to perform a novel undertaking. It is, to speak the truth of William Hazlitt. This writer has been praised more than he deserves; and yet not enough. And he has been abused more than he or than any man deserves; and yet his faults have never been pointed out. In short,

* This paper was for obvious reasons " rejected" from a late publication, entitled The Spirit of the Age ; and it was, I suppose for the same reasons, refused admission into the amusing periodical in which a portion of that work had previously appeared. I feel peculiar satisfaction in being able to present this paper to the public ;—first, because it is more than probable that, but for this particular medium, it would-never have seen the light at all ; and secondly, because there can be no doubt whatever, in regard to the person whose portrait is here drawn, that, as " none but himself can be his parallel," so none but himself either can or dare give a true account of him.—*Editor.*

he has been praised and abused through thick and thin; but he has never yet been *estimated.* He shall be so now, as nearly as we are able to do it.

We have had some doubts about placing Mr. Hazlitt's portrait among those whose intellects make up " The Spirit of the Age ;" because strictly speaking none are entitled to that rank who have not positively and directly contributed to create that spirit, or are pretty sure sooner or later to do so: and Mr. Hazlitt neither has nor ever will.   But we could not persuade ourselves to exclude him from a company of which we ˙have thought Jeoffry Crayon, and two or three others who shall be equally nameless, not unworthy to come among the number.

If a better reason than the above is desired, all we have to give is, that if Mr. Hazlitt has not set his mark upon the Age in which he lives, it is his own fault.   He might have done it if he would, and in signs and characters that those who run might read.   It is a sufficient misfortune to his Age and to himself that he has not done so, and will not, without its being made an excuse for depriving our readers of a portrait that they will probably look for with some curiosity, if it is only in expectation of the abuse that they have so long

been accustomed to see connected with his name ;
Mr. Hazlitt being for the most part known only
through the medium of the Quarterly Review
and Blackwood's Magazine.   And by the bye, that
abuse itself, reaching us through the above-named
mediums, may be offered as tolerably conclusive
collateral evidence that we are not doing any great
wrong in placing Mr. Hazlitt's name in our list ;
for the person whom those publications " delight
to *dis*honour," may be safely pronounced to be no
insignificant one at least.   But let us " leave this
face-making, and begin."

No writer ever acquired marked distinction in
his day, of whose writings something might not be
said, either in relation to kind or to degree, which
could not be said of any others whatever.   And
perhaps this is the best criterion that can be
given, to determine who is and who is not entitled
to rank among the Spirits of the Age in which he
lives.   In regard to Mr. Hazlitt's writings, this
one distinguishing quality is the unrivalled power
which they display of looking into the hidden
truth of things.   He pierces the depths of human
life, and " plucks out the heart of their mystery."
His pen is like Ithuriel's spear; whatever it touches
starts up before us in its naked truth.   If you are

afraid to hear the truth you must not listen to him ; for it *will* out, whatever may be the consequences. And this even when the truth in question is a personal one. But when it is an abstract truth that he happens to hit upon, " away at once with love and jealousy!" out it must come, even though it should blacken his dearest friend or brighten his bitterest foe ; for the truth is to him —the truth.

Perhaps it may be said that the leading feature of Mr. Hazlitt's mind—that which constitutes its great strength as well as its great weakness—is this passion which he cherishes, to the exclusion of all others, for abstract truth; for his other passion, for Liberty, is but a branch or off-set of this. He would not scruple, upon occasion, to tell a lie, out of pure love for the truth ! just as he would assist in making himself and everybody else slaves in practice, out of his love for Liberty in the abstract. This may seem paradoxical, but it is capable of an easy explanation. He has a *catholic* zeal for the truth ; and though he would not die a martyr to it in a bodily sense, (for we venture to guess that he is constitutionally timid in regard to bodily suffering), yet he would not scruple to sacrifice his principles to it, and his

sense of practical justice : just as a lover is
always fonder of his passion than of his mistress,
and would at any time sacrifice the latter to the
former.

A consequence of Mr. Hazlitt's indestructible
passion for abstract truth is, the absolutely un-
changeable nature of all his opinions. With
him a thing either *is,* or *is not ;* and there is
no disputing about it.   He would even interpret
literally the old axiom, *De gustibus non est dis-
putandum,* and insist that a man either *has* a taste
for truth and beauty, or he has it not ; and that
he who prefers falsehood and deformity, or even
the lesser degree of beauty to the greater, does so
not because he sees with-another eye, but because
he does not see at all ; not because his faculties
are different, but because they are defective. If you
tell him, for example, that you prefer a picture of
Correggio's to one of Raphael's, he will not let you
off in virtue of the above maxim ; though he is
too modest a man to be the first to dispute the
point with you.   But if you are imprudent
enough to insist on " giving *a reason* for the faith
that is in you," then the chances are that he will
not only prove but proclaim you a fool for your
pains.

It has been said of Cobbett, that he has not one Mrs. Cobbett among all his opinions. It may in the same manner be said of Hazlitt, that he has no one opinion which is *not* a Mrs. Hazlitt. He was wedded to every one of them in his youth, and he has stuck to them ever since, " through good report and through evil report."   Not but what we believe he would be very glad to be divorced from some of them *à mensa et thoro* ; for if we may judge from some parts of his writings, they lead him a sad life between them ; particularly those of them that trouble their heads about Politics.   But it is no easy matter to make up one's mind to part for ever from a wife that one loves, however ill she may treat us, or whatever we may be forced to suffer through her follies or extravagancies.   And perhaps the more wives a man has, the less inducement he feels for getting rid of any one that he may be suffering by.   In Turkey, where a man may have as many as he pleases, the law of divorce is a dead letter.

But besides these considerations, Mr. Hazlitt has a conscience, touching his intellectual ties, however he may feel himself too poor to afford to keep one in other matters.   He took his opinions " for better for worse ;" and he cannot now persuade himself to kick them out of doors merely because with their youth they may have lost some of their pristine freshness and beauty. One thing we will say in his favour on this head ; (and it even makes up for all the faults that have been imputed to him, much more for those which he actually possesses) : it is this—if some of the opinions to which he is wedded have long been " the plague of his life," and he would fain have been without them in an honest way, he has never yet been base enough to connive at their prostituting themselves, in order that he might make that an excuse for getting quit of them!

To escape at once from this long-winded metaphor,—Mr. Hazlitt commenced his career as a thinker, (though not as an author), at that period which produced several more of the most distinguished writers of the day. He was, at the breaking out of the French Revolution, one of a band of youthful enthusiasts, who implicitly believed in all the moral truth and beauty which that event held forth the hopes of, and who were all acted upon by it in an equal *degree*, though all in a different *manner*. We allude, besides Mr. Hazlitt, to his then friends, Messrs. Wordsworth,

Coleridge, Southey, and Dr. Stoddart. This associated band of intellectual brothers included a few more names; but these are the only ones which have since become distingushed.

Upon Mr. Wordsworth this event acted but as a confirmation of his preconceived notions touching the nature and destiny of man. If Mr. Wordsworth is the most philosophical of poets, or the most poetical of philosophers, (which you will), he is even more of a philosopher than a poet. This event, therefore, was for him only a natural and necessary corollary from the premises to which he had early made up his mind; and it moved him no jot from " the even tenor of his way." He wrote ballads, then, about Alice Fells and Idiot Boys, just as he writes them about Peter Bells and Waggoners, now, that all his bright hopes have blasted in the bud by the pestiferous breath of the hag Legitimacy, which he and his friends in their mistaken humanity helped to escape with her life, instead of, as they ought, treading her black blood and rotten bones into the soil which she had so long polluted, or burning them in a great *auto da fé* on the altar of human liberty, and scattering their ashes to the four winds of heaven, amid shouts of holy exultation that the angels themselves might have listened to on their thrones of light.

But Mr. Wordsworth is a philanthropist as well as a philosopher; and we must not wonder, therefore, if he was willing to connive at sparing the lives of half a dozen kings; though his boasted philosophy might have taught him that it must be done at the cost of those of millions upon millions of their subjects; to say nothing of that of Liberty herself—which is worth them all!

The personal consequences to Mr. Wordsworth have been exactly what they ought:—he is patronized by Lord Lonsdale, praised by Mr. Gifford, and paid out of the pockets of the people!

On Mr. Coleridge the effects of the French Revolution and its failure were as different as the different nature of the two minds on which they were to operate.   Mr. Coleridge lives but in dreams of poetry, and mystic revelations from other worlds; and this event promised to be the parent of such dreams and revelations as had not till then visited the mind of man.   What then could he do, when all these " gorgeous palaces " of our intellectual pride, these " solemn temples " of our human hopes and affections, were either levelled with the dust and their golden images broken in pieces and trodden under foot, or (still worse) turned into marts for money-changers and dens for thieves; and when all the fairy fabric had melted away (as it soon afterwards did) " like breath into the wind;" what, we say, could Mr. Coleridge be expected to do under such circumstances, but " wink, and shut his apprehension up " for a brief space, and then sink into that listless state, between sleeping and waking, in which he has remained ever since?

And yet Coleridge was the wisest of the set, after all; or at any rate he was the happiest; which is much the same thing. Until the French Revolution came, he knew of nothing better in the world than his own talk about his own fancies; and when it ceased to exist it left him just where it found him. He had done nothing but talk before; (and how could he do better, considering what his talk is?) and he has done nothing else since. And the only difference its failure has made to him is, that he has one more subject to talk about: which indeed he would if it had succeeded; so that to him it has made no difference at all.

Alas! not so to Mr. Southey. The breaking out of the French Revolution found *him* " a poet," in the purest and loftiest sense of that pure and lofty title. And its failure has left him—a Poet-laureat! Ill betide those who caused that failure, if for nothing but for this alone! The French Revolution came upon Mr. Southey like a flash of lightning breaking over a traveller in sight of a nobly extended prospect at midnight; not only revealing for a moment to his half benighted senses a thousand objects that he had not even hoped to see, but decking them all in a beauty not their own. Alas! where is that prospect now! "Whither is fled the glory and the dream?" No wonder, when the sky closed again, and made all by the contrast seem ten times darker than it was before—no wonder that the author of Wat Tyler and Joan of Arc should wilfully shut his eyes upon the scene, and after wandering about for a while amidst the dreary darkness, find himself at last walking up the steps of Carlton Palace, with a dress sword by his side, an opera hat under his arm, and a copy of the Quarterly Review and the Vision of Judgment sticking out of each pocket of his cut velvet coat!

Foul befal those (we repeat it) who brought about that bitter change! For all the other changes which that fatal blow to the hopes of human liberty brought with it, we could have found "some drop of patience;" because all

N

the others, if they were not anticipated, might have been.

> " But *there*, where we had garnered up our hearts !
>   To be discarded thence—
>   Or keep it as a cistern for foul *toryism*
>   To knot and gender in !
>   Patience, thou young and rose-lipped cherubim,
>   Turn thy complexion there, ay, there look grim
>   As hell !"

But no more of this.

It is not worth while to inquire what were the changes wrought on the then unknown, but since notorious Dr. Stoddart, by the great event we have alluded to ; for it is true (though Mr. Croker has said it) that " once a Jacobin always a Jacobin ;" and the Editor of the Old and New Times was never anything better. He took up the trade then because it gave him an opportunity of indulging his natural disposition to blacken his betters ; and he has laid it by for that of Editor of a Tory newspaper, for the same reason. How this person contrives to live at all, now that he who was lately, even while bound to his barren rock, " the foremost man of all this world," is laid in his lowly grave, and no longer a butt for the poisoned arrows of his filthy abuse, is more than we can imagine. Probably he consoles himself with the soothing reflection that *he* assisted in sending him there.

So much for the effect of the French Revolution on the early associates of Mr. Hazlitt. On himself it worked a change less noticeable than on his friends, but more worthy of notice. It found him still a youth, and his youthful faculties, however prematurely developed in some respects, more than proportionately backward in others. He was a reasoner and a metaphysician even then ; but he was not then what he soon afterwards became— a man of deep sensibility, of a most vigorous and profound if not an excursive imagination, and a fancy active and vivacious in the highest degree.

The event in question promised to realize all the conclusions, in regard to the fitness of things, and their conformity with natural truth and justice, which Mr. Hazlitt's logical understanding had at that time enabled him to reach. And these promises so far exceeded any *hopes* that he could have previously entertained, (for his temperament is anything but sanguine,) that they must have produced an instantaneous and an almost miraculous effect, in developing those other faculties which

N 2

we have ascribed to him, and which are usually
so seldom allied to extraordinary powers of reason-
ing.   But, however this may be, those other faculties *were* developed about this time; the early
successes of the good cause urged them forward
in their course, and impelled them to a pitch of
almost diseased activity; and then, in the midst
of all this tumult of irrepressible exultation at the
re-appearance of those hopes of human liberty
which had for so many ages been hidden in the
secret hearts of a few lone enthusiasts—in the
midst of this came crime, and bloodshed, and
shame; and then an instinctive combination of
all the bad of the earth against all the good ;
and at last the consequent triumph of the former,
as they always must triumph while the latter
refuse to avail themselves of the same ways and
the same weapons.   If the *people* of the earth
had felt no more remorse at shedding *drops* of
blood than its *kings* did and do at shedding *oceans*,
all would have been well, and that people would not
have seen their own blood poured forth like water,
and their miseries laughed to scorn.   As it is, they
have more than half deserved their fate.

But what must have been the effect of all this
on a mind like Mr. Hazlitt's?   We must not
dwell upon the picture.   Suffice it to say, that

" He, repulsed, (a short tale to make)
   Fell into a sadness—then into a fast—
   Thence into a watch—then into a weakness—
   Thence to a lightness ; and by this declension
   Into the madness wherein he *(sometimes)* raves
   And we all mourn for."

But let us not forget to mention one thing. To
Mr. Hazlitt's eternal honour be it spoken, whatever
else the failure of all his hopes and aspirations made
of him, it did not make him an apostate. And
which of his early friends, " all honourable men" as
they are, can say as much ? Because those hopes
were blasted in their bloom, and lost the odour of
their sweetness, *he* did not turn round upon them
with a feigned contempt, and after " casting them
like loathsome weeds away," fling himself at the
feet of the blasters. Because his arm was too
weak to overthrow the car of the great Juggernaut,
Legitimacy, *he* did not basely cast himself beneath
its blood-stained wheels—a willing sacrifice to the
object of his execrations. Because he found from
fatal experience that man was *not* made to be only
" a little lower than the angels," *he* did not lend a
helping hand to put harness on his back, and sink
him to a lower level than that of the brutes that
perish. In short, because Liberty, the betrothed
of his early hopes, the divinity of his youthful
adoration, proved false and " haggard," *he* did

not " cast her off to beggarly divorcement," and thus prove that it was not her but himself he was loving all the while; but he clung to her more closely the more she was deserted by others; and fallen and polluted as she is, has worshipped her with a religious idolatry ever since. Let but this one truth be written on his tomb-stone, and with all his faults, (of which he has his full share), his name shall be repeated with respect when those of his ci-devant friends " stink in the nostrils of posterity."

Those friends may say, perhaps, that he has not been tempted like them, or like them he would have fallen. But this is begging the question with a vengeance; or worse—it is stealing it. No sophistry can annul the vital difference that exists between them. It is a matter of bare fact, and it stands simply thus : *they* abandoned the principles on which they commenced their career, the moment it became dangerous and unprofitable to hold them ; and *he* has held by them manfully to the last. In a word, they *are* apostates, and he *is not*.

But " something too much of this." It would not have been introduced at all here, if the circumstances immediately connected with it had not produced a marked effect on the intellectual

features of the person whose portrait we are attempting to sketch. The French Revolution rose like a beautiful meteor, only to dazzle the eye for a moment, and then to set in blood; and with it set for ever the momentary hopes of our young searcher after truth. And as their last rays receded from his eyes upon the distant horizon, and he saw at the same time his early friends and companions—men to whom he had looked up with the most unfeigned reverence—falling down in ignoble worship before the idols that were rising from the earth in an opposite direction, a black and baleful melancholy seemed to be settling within his heart; a cherished distrust in his fellow men took possession of his imagination; an indignant scowl seated itself upon his magnificent brow, (like a demon usurping the throne that was erected for a god); a pallid languor hung upon his cheeks and lips, and dragged them downwards; his shoulders became bowed and bent as if a world of disappointments were resting and pressing upon them; and he went wandering about among his fellow men, as he has done ever since, in loose attire, a shambling gait, and a sinister look, the very picture of a man possessed by a spirit of mingled hatred and contempt for all the world, and most of all for himself.

This is a sorry picture to be obliged to draw, of a man towards whom we feel as we do towards Mr. Hazlitt. But we promised our readers the truth, and it shall be told. And at any rate *he* will not be the person to complain of it; for, to say nothing of his being the most bold and reckless truth-teller of the day, he has still one love left :— his passion for truth is not yet extinguished, and he will bear to hear it with equanimity even of himself.

If it should be said that we have dwelt too long on the merely personal part of our picture, we could not help it. It is a theme that *will* have its way, when it comes across us. We must endeavour to make up for our transgression in what follows.

We have said that the most distinguishing feature of Mr. Hazlitt's mind, as displayed in his writings, is its unrivalled power of piercing into the truth. When there is nothing, either from without or from within, to affect the natural powers of his vision, perhaps, to use a vulgar phrase, he " sees farther into the mill-stone" than any man that ever lived. But on the other hand, there is this to be said of him : he frequently sees farther into it than its proper thickness; he sees more than is to be seen.

We are willing to believe that this results, in most cases, from his determination to say striking things. He writes for his bread. (We need not scruple to say here what we learn from those writings themselves.) He writes for his bread; and therefore he must write what people will read. If the subject on which he happens to be writing is capable of a popular development consistently with truth, well and good ; but it must *have* one at all events. If he determines that half a dozen brilliant things must be said on a given topic, and only three present themselves naturally, three more must be made. " Be brilliant,"—is his business maxim in these matters ; in conformity with reason and common-sense if you can ; but— be brilliant.

It is astonishing the mischievous effect this has produced upon his writings ; and if nothing should hereafter occur to induce him to care more about his reputation than he at present seems to do, or look better after it while he lives, when he dies it will not be strong enough to take care of itself. If the profound and subtle truths, and the admirable illustrations and applications of them, scattered about at random through half a dozen of Mr. Hazlitt's volumes, had made their appearance in a well-concocted form in one, that

whom he feels but a slender portion of respect
lends him a hundred pounds when he could have
little expected it, he proclaims him in his next
volume, " the prince of critics, and the king of
men." And if another, whom he perhaps *does* respect, passes him in the street without seeing him,
he writes him down " a rascal" on the very first
opportunity that offers. If Mr. Hazlitt says, as
perhaps he may, that if self-preservation is the
first law of nature, gratitude and revenge are the
second and third, and that if you cannot have
them in one way, you must in another—we shall
not dispute it. All we say is, that such a mode
of achieving them leads him into the most ridiculous dilemmas ; besides taking away from his
writings that " broad and general air" which
should belong to them, and making them

> " —— cabinned, cribbed, confined,
> Bound in to *saucy doubts and fears.*"

Mr. Hazlitt is one of those rare writers who
teach you what, *but for them,* you never would have
known : and this we take to be the true criterion
of genius, in whatever department of human inquiry it may be found. Some of the moral truths

which he has stated and developed would have remained for ever among the hidden secrets of nature, if he had not lived to draw them forth. We do not of course mean to state that it required a *degree* of mental power never attained before, to enable him to produce certain portions of his writings. What we mean is, that it required precisely *that* degree which is possessed by him, added to his other qualities of sensibility, excitability, &c. and that these together amount to what we consent to call *genius*. Without anything like this degree of mental power, he might have been quite as lively, as brilliant, and as popular a writer as he is; and if we are obliged to add quite as useful, it is because he has chosen, not absolutely to *mis*apply those powers, but to leave them *un*applied. But still, without precisely *that* degree of capacity possessed by him, and unless that degree had amounted to genius, he could not have done certain things that he *has* done.

This leads us to state what is perhaps the most distinguishing fact connected with Mr. Hazlitt as a prose writer of the nineteenth century. He is the only one of them all whose powers do amount to genius: we mean, those who have addicted themselves to prose exclusively; for we are not aware that Mr. Hazlitt has ever written a line of poetry, except in his prose.

By the bye, we take this to be a singular fact; though one that it would perhaps be not very difficult to account for. Mr. Hazlitt has displayed as enthusiastic a passion for poetry, and as acute a judgment and delicate a sensibility in detecting its beauties, as any one of his cotemporaries. There is a maxim, too, which is pretty generally admitted, that " none but a poet can criticise a poet." And yet Mr. Hazlitt has never attempted a line of poetry himself. The reason is this : he has never written poetry, because he is able to *think* it, and *feel* it, just as well *without* writing it : for as to his writing poetry, or any thing else, with a direct view to any one's benefit but his own—that is entirely out of the question with him ; partly from a selfish indifference to the good of others, which has been superinduced on his natural disposition by the events of his early life ; but chiefly, we verily believe, from a shrewd suspicion, that if " a great book is a great evil," a small one is only so much the less evil. But however this may be, perhaps, no poem was ever yet written that it might be read. Poets write because their faculties require the stimulus of composition, before they can reach

that state of excitement in which their being, as
poets, consists ;—they sit down to write, not because they *are* poets at the moment, but in order
that they may become such.   If it were not for
this, heaven knows, those who are *not* poets would
have little chance of enjoying any of those
feelings which poetry excites ; at least, so long
as the market price of poetry remains, generally
speaking, infinitely below that of prose, in proportion to the time required for its production.
We conceive Mr. Hazlitt's imagination to be
so intense, his fancy so active, and his sensibility so acute, that he sees poetry in everything, and feels it at all times ; and *therefore*,
he never writes it.   Let any bookseller pay
him fifty guineas (beforehand !) for five hundred
lines of poetry, and see if he will not produce them.
But otherwise, why should he, when he can get
four times the sum for as many pages of prose
that would hardly cost him more time ? *

* We would wish our readers to take this speculation *cum
grano salis*, so far as regards those who *have* written poetry in
the present day.   We will not pretend to state it as our belief
that all the vast mass of our cotemporary poetry was written
purely for the immediate pleasure of writing it ; and assuredly,
very little of it was written for the money that was to be made
by it.   No doubt, the motive which produced the greater part of
it was triple—present pleasure, profit, and reputation.   So far

It is not generally known that Mr. Hazlitt studied Painting for several years, and practised as an artist; and that he has executed some copies from Titian which are looked upon by pretty good judges as among the best that have ever been done after that master—whom it is almost as difficult to copy as to rival. But though no one else was dis-satisfied with the progress he made in Painting, he himself was. He did not see *why* he should be inferior *to* any man; and when he found that he *was* so, he threw up his pencil in disgust, and has never touched it since.

He then came to London, and was engaged as Parliamentary reporter for some of the daily

as relates to Mr. Hazlitt himself our speculation rests on the express understanding that his motive to write is profit alone.* Not that he is careless about reputation. No man of fine genius ever was. He is even greedy of it, and would enjoy no small share if it could be had merely for the trouble of wishing for. But he is utterly incapable of *acting* with a direct and immediate view to its acquirement.

---

* If the reader should detect some little inconsistency between this passage and another at p. 190, where the writer says that the subject of his notice does not write poetry " because he is able to *think* it and *feel* it just as well *without* writing it," he must not complain of *me*, at least. I am not editor enough to pretend to make these articles better than I find them. Still less do I offer a selection of the " beauties" of our popular prose writers. I give the matter just as it comes to hand—adhering with strictness even to the punctuation.—*Editor.*

papers.   From this laborious but useful drudgery
he was *promoted* to purveyor of theatrical critiques,
and other occasional paragraphs;   in which his
power of thought and of style soon shone out in a
manner not a little marvellous in the eyes of those
who had hitherto looked to the Morning Post for
their beau-ideal of such matters.   There can be
little doubt that we owe almost entirely to him
the present tone of our theatrical criticism,—which
is not absolutely contemptible ; whereas, at the
time we speak of, it was infinitely below contempt.

About the same time, too, or shortly after, he
began writing under the form of essays, in weekly
papers ; (chiefly, we believe, the Examiner) ; and
evinced a boldness and originality of thought, and
a spirit and vigour of style, that excited consider-
able attention among a certain class of readers,
but much less than they deserved generally, on account of an evidently careless, not to say insolent
disregard of the commonly received opinions of the
day, which accompanied almost all he put forth.
When an important truth occurred to him, he did
not, any more than he does now, tender it politely
for your examination, finically folded up in a
genteel wrapper of gentle phrases, as if he was

o

afraid it might contaminate your touch; but he flung it in its simple nakedness, right in the face of the most deep-rooted prejudice of the day, or the most wide-spread interest; and if those whom it concerned did not like to pick it up, they might leave it.   When he was determined to make war upon a well-bred lie, or a fashionably attired sophistry, he did not send a friend to call upon it, provided with a politely penned challenge, written on hot-pressed and gilt-edged paper, and sealed with his coat of arms; but he flung his mailed glove smack down before it wherever he happened to meet it, and dared it once " to the outrance."

Soon after this, Mr. Hazlitt was engaged to give Lectures on English poetry, at the Surry Institution, which were afterwards published in a collected form.   This brought him much more into public notice than he had hitherto been; though in the literary world he had for some time past been pretty generally looked upon as a person of first-rate ability.   But while it gained him many admirers that he would not otherwise have met with, by presenting his opinions in a tangible and cognizable form, it placed him at the mercy of those who have no mercy, much less justice, when the paltry interests of their employers are threatened from the remotest distance with invasion, or even with examination.

What followed is too well known to need repetition here. Mr. Hazlitt has ever since been the butt and byeword of all the base hirelings of the day; from the editor of the Quarterly Review, downwards, or upwards — which you will,—for there is not a pin to choose between them, in literary rank any more than in moral respectability. On every successive publication he has been assailed by the mingled hootings and execrations of those who have no other honours to bestow.

Let it not be supposed that we refer to this fact under any affected feelings of pity or deprecation. Mr. Hazlitt is among the last persons in the world to claim exemption, when the *lex talionis* is the order of the day—as it is at present; for no one ever stood less nice than he does about taking the exact measurement of personal merit in a political adversary, or of awarding precisely the deserved number of blows to any unfortunate delinquent of this sort who may happen to fall into his hands. So far from it, he seems to think all fair in politics, whatever he may in love; and when he is in the mood for it, would as soon call Mr. Wordsworth a knave as he would Mr. Theodore Hook.

We merely refer to the unmeasured abuse that
has been heaped on Mr. Hazlitt, as a striking sign
of the Spirit of the Age. We firmly believe, indeed, that *he* would have fallen into this error in
regard to others, in whatever age he had lived;
because it is a vice of his blood, and he can no
more help it than he can help dashing his racket
or his head against the wall when he makes a bad
stroke at the Fives Court, or in fact than any of
us can help losing our temper when we *do* lose it.
In him, therefore, we can in some sort excuse it;
though we would on no account seek to exempt
him from the consequence which such a weakness
entails. But perhaps he is the only reckless
abuser of his day for whom this excuse (such as
it is) can be made. *He* vituperates the objects of
his political hatred in terms that they do not always deserve, because, when that hatred is stirred
up to its height, he neither knows nor cares for
the precise value of the terms he uses. But with
the systematic maligners of the day it is a very different matter. *They* do not even murder reputation with " malice prepense;" for they have not
heart or gall enough to be " haters " at all, much
less such a " good hater " as he piques himself on
being. They commit their moral assassinations
as the Italian bravos do,—for hire; and have no

more enmity to the person they seek to destroy,
than they have love to the cause or the party
they serve. With them it is an affair of pure calculation, and they sit down to consider of it as
coolly as they would to a sum in arithmetic.
Will it pay to poison the public mind against such
or such a person ? Is he of sufficient importance
to make it prudent to do so ? Will the reprisals he
is likely to make leave a balance in favour of our
party ? These are the kind of questions they ask
themselves—or when not authorised to act on
their own judgment, their employers. And if the
answers are in the affirmative, they next proceed
to enquire into the actual character, both mental
and moral, of the person to be put down ; and
whatever that may be, regulate their attack accordingly. For example, if the peculiar characteristics of his mind happen to be subtlety and
acuteness, they swear that he is an ass ; if he is
particularly remarkable for modesty and diffidence
of deportment, they write him up a bully and a
Bobadil; if they should happen to learn (by means
of their spies) that he never drinks any thing but
water, they instantly offer to prove that he gets drunk
every morning upon gin and bitters, and every night
upon brandy-punch ; and so of the rest. Nay, it
is not without example, when nothing else seemed

likely to do, for them to throw out pretty broad
insinuations, the nature of which cannot even be
insinuated here!

But they have another method, which is a still
greater favourite with them than any of the
preceding, and not without reason, for it is in
some cases more effective than any other.   It
consists in the artillery of nick-names.   A nick-
name is at once irresistible and unanswerable.
It is a dab of moral mud thrown at a man.   If
thrown skilfully it is sure to stick, and if it sticks
it is sure to make the bearer of it look ridiculous.
If the first nobleman or the finest gentleman in
the land were to walk along London Streets with
a great dab of mud upon his cheek, the very
chimney-sweepers would laugh and " point the
finger " at him as he passed.   And precisely so it
is with a nick-name.   There is no gainsaying it.
It is worse than an " *ill*-name ;" and those who
give it might as well swear away a man's life at
once, and have him hanged outright.   And so they
would if they dared.

But these gentry are leading us farther from
our subject than it is either worth while or decent
to follow them.   What we were about to say was,
that this kind of warfare is one of those signs
which mark the Spirit of the Age.   Extremes meet ;

and we are now arrived at that extreme pitch of refinement which merges into barbarism. In no other age would the kind of warfare we have alluded to been tolerated; and it is tolerated now, only because

" We have given our hearts away—a sordid boon ;"

and are pretty much in that moral condition in which men are before they have hearts to give.

Oh, it was not so once! Alas! whither are ye fled, white years of youth! Beautiful hopes of opening life, why are ye changed to blank misgivings, and base suspicions, and coward fears, and constant uncontrollable perturbations, that prey upon the pierced spirit like canker-worms, and will not let it rest! It is but a little while, and that spirit was wandering like a bird beside the ever-sounding sea ; as pure as the air that seemed to lift it from the earth ; as clear as the waters over which it floated at will, or plunged into their green depths in search of unimagined wonders ; as free and unconfined as the space in which it expatiated, or turned by a thought into the temple of its triumphant worship! What and where is it now ? A denizen of that world which it loathes, yet dares not leave;—a declaimer in favour of that virtue it has forfeited and that sincerity it has flung away;—a sophisticator with that truth which it still professes to idolize;—and (oh shame of shames!) ready to truckle at the footstool of that power which it would fain see sunk into the central fires of the earth that it outrages and pollutes!

We shall not detain our readers by any lengthened details in regard to works now so well known as the characters of Shakespeare's Plays, the Lectures on the English Poets, and the Table Talk. They are each " of a mingled yarn—good and ill"—as what book is not? each contains numerous examples of all the faults that we have attributed to this writer, and all his good qualities; and all are what they were perhaps intended to be more than any thing else,—infinitely entertaining; and the last named—the two volumes of Table Talk—are perhaps more so than any other volumes of the day. For our own parts we would even go the length of making no exception whatever to this remark. We do not of course mean to assert that people hurry through them with that eager interest with which they devour the Scotch Novels; or that a tenth part so many persons look into them at all. But those who do read them turn to them ten times after the first perusal, for once that they turn to the others. And to say nothing of their

readers being of the only class worthy that name, they are nearly all *buyers* of them ; which very few are indeed of the novels, compared with the enormous number that is sold.	The chief consumers of the latter are the circulating libraries, and those numerous little *lending shops* which they have created in every large town throughout the kingdom.	There are circulating libraries in London that are obliged to have from fifty to seventy copies of each novel when it comes out.	And those who actually buy them on their first appearance, merely to read, are chiefly those who have plenty of money and little patience, and therefore chuse to pay a guinea and a half for an early perusal.	And this includes the additional advantage of being able to lend them to friend after friend, till they are fairly lost, and you are exempted from the task of taking them up again ! for delightful as it is the first time, it is felt to be a task afterwards.

But with the Table Talk it is different.	The real readers of the day are comparatively very few.	And of these every one is a buyer, to a certain extent.	There are a few books—one or two in a season or so—that they *must* have. Now if the little libraries of these real lovers of books were searched, with a view to ascertain the comparative popularity of any given prose writer of the day, we would venture odds that Mr. Hazlitt would carry it hollow against them all. And we would *take* odds that the Table Talk would, like Roderick Random (was it not?) in the ten Carlton-house lists of books supposed to be the most entertaining in the English language, be included in them all!

The reader will perceive that, according to this calculation, (or speculation, if he pleases) the popularity of a book is in an inverse ratio to its sale! But though as a general proposition this would be ridiculously untrue, it is nothing less in the particular instance in question. Nay—it may be added—(and the *rationale* of the proposition may be found in what has been said above)—that if the Scotch Novels were read ten times as often as they are by the same persons who now read them, there would not be half so many of them sold. So that the author of them must take care what he is about, and not write them too well, lest he should get more of the " empty praise" of admiration in part payment of his demands, and less of that " solid pudding" which is evidently so much more palatable to him. Not

that he needs any hint of this kind from us.
Indeed he seems to have been acting on this feeling of late, to a somewhat ominous extreme !

We have but little more to say of Mr. Hazlitt,
and his works. The most remarkable feature of
his style is, that there is no remarkable feature
belonging to it. He studiously avoids the use of
uncommon and obsolete words ; and never uses
a common word in an uncommon sense. But
perhaps it would be impossible to give a just
account of what his style would seem to *aim at
being,* without repeating, almost in so many words,
what he has himself said in describing his notion of
" The Familiar Style." We must therefore refer
the reader to that essay, in the second volume of
Table Talk. How far it is conformable with that
notion, is another question. In some particular
instances, and where he has *taken pains* to make
it so, (as for example in the Essay itself just referred to), we take it to be the very best specimen
of that style extant; and we agree with him in
thinking that style the best. But generally
speaking it falls short of what it aims at being ;
or rather it goes beyond. It is frequently so
idiomatical as to be quite enigmatical, to all but
those who are *up to* the slang of the last quarter

of a century.   It is sometimes so very "familiar" that it "breeds contempt."   Its plainness often borders on ugliness.   In avoiding anything like an oratorical construction, it is frequently broken into bits.   Its periods have no more words than some writers have clauses.   It is anything but long-winded.   It seems to be written for persons afflicted with asthma.   You may read it aloud while smoking your cigar; puff and paragraph, alternately.   Not that we would recommend this practice : for though not professors of it ourselves, we should conceive that smoking, like painting, requires the whole man.

We should venture to judge that if Mr. Hazlitt's choice of the familiar style in the first instance was the result of his naturally pure taste, he has adhered to it so long on account of the facilities it has afforded him ; for, as we before hinted, he does not pretend to keep a conscience in so purely a matter of business as authorship now is with him.   On the contrary, whatever serves the turn of the moment is welcome. Forced conceits and hacknied quotations ; paltry points, staring paradoxes, and petty plays on words ; scraps of Latin and French picked up nobody or everybody knows where ;   anthitheses, alliterations, and any other helps and make-weights, however unmeaning and meretricious, (including the whole family of the *Gingles*)—all are laid under contribution whenever they present themselves. He is far from particular : if " my lady" is not to be had, he is content with " Joan." In short, in this respect, " nought is for him too high, and nought too low."

Again—when he sets himself to make out a case, if he cannot do it by fair means he will do it by foul ; or he will frequently do whichever is easiest, or whichever will *tell* best. And why not ? He writes that you may " read ;" but not that you may " mark, learn, and inwardly digest." Or, putting it in another point of view,—he cannot afford to give you more than a little of the " leaven" of wisdom to each " lump" (" abortions" he has himself called them) that he periodically lays before you ; otherwise what is to become of all those which he must produce during the next twenty years ? But this does not belong to style.

Mr. Hazlitt's metaphors, figures, and what are usually considered as the higher parts of style, frequently " come as tardy off" as his language and construction. They are very seldom inapt ; but they run upon one, two, three, or four feet, as it may happen. And no wonder, considering the distance from which some of them are fetched.

So much for the defects of Mr. Hazlitt's style. Its merits must not be dwelt upon so long in proportion, or the rest of the Spirit of the Age " must halt for it." We will only say that when he is in earnest in his endeavour to develop a truth, or anxious in his attempt to disentangle a difficulty, or unaffectedly impelled to pour forth a burst of passion, or sincerely eager to impress an opinion, or deeply interested in establishing a theory or illustrating a theme,—there is no one like him. Then his power of style is equal to his power of thought and penetration,—which are unrivalled. Then he can shoot forth winged words like arrows; each following each to its destination, and no one impeding another. Then he can link simile to simile, and place figure beside figure, and pile metaphor upon metaphor, till each illustrates each, and all melt into one mellow whole, like the parts of a beautiful picture. Then he can make fancy beget fancy, and draw imagination from imagination, and support truth against truth, and multiply argument into argument, and distil sentiment out of sentiment,—till there is neither power nor will left in the reader to gainsay or resist him. In short, then, and then only, he is that really admirable expounder of truth, and detector and destroyer of falsehood, which he might always be if he pleased.

As we have mentioned the conversational powers of some other of the subjects of our remarks, it would scarcely be fair towards Mr. Hazlitt entirely to pass over his. Perhaps if Mr. Coleridge is, among professedly literary men, the best *talker* of his day, Mr. Hazlitt is upon the whole the best *converser ;* which is better—for it is calculated to give more immediate pleasure to his fellow conversers than ever Mr. C.'s can to his *hearers,* while it is pretty sure to be of more after benefit to them. We will venture to say of Mr. Hazlitt's conversation, that it includes *every* one of the good qualities of his writings, and *not* one of their faults. And the reasons are simply these : he is fond of talking, whereas he hates writing; and in talking, he is not called upon to say more than he *has* to say, whereas in writing he frequently is—having engaged to fill a certain space on a certain topic. In short, he talks with perfect sincerity and good faith ; thinking whatever he says, and saying whatever he thinks. But he writes, as it may happen : what he thinks, if he thinks that will *do :* if not, anything that will.

We must now take leave of Mr. Hazlitt, and

abruptly, for we have long passed our limits.   We
shall do so by saying, that whenever he pleases to
take the trouble, he may approve himself to all
the world, what two of the best judges in it have
already pronounced him——the best prose writer of
his day, and one of the finest spirits of his age
and country.*

* Hear (if you can) Lord Holland's conversation ; and see a
Letter of Mr. Charles Lamb to Mr. Southey, printed some time
ago in the London Magazine.

LONDON LETTERS

TO

COUNTRY COUSINS.

P

LONDON LETTERS

TO

COUNTRY COUSINS.

No. 5.*

THE STREETS OF LONDON BY GAS-LIGHT.

I INTENDED, my dear Frank, (or rather, my dear
cousins conjointly—for this epistle is addressed to
all of you,) to have delayed offering you any *general* sketches of London in 1825, till I had prepared
you for their due appreciation, by placing before
you a few more of its particular features. But as
I hear from authentic sources, that certain evil
disposed persons are, at this present writing, engaged in laying a deep hatched and deadly plot,
against the very existence of what I had intended
should form one of the most characteristic and
attractive of, my themes, I must pounce upon it

* Continued from New Monthly Magazine—p. 132 of the
Number for August, 1825.

at once, before it passes into a thing that was ;—
seeing that it is the very essence of these agreeable
missives, to make you acquainted with nothing but
what actually is ; leaving what has been to those
who have been, and what is to be, to those who
are not.

You must know, that it has been the laudable
practice of the principal London linen-drapers,
and a few other retail tradesmen, time immemorial,
(that is to say for these ten years past,) to keep
open their shops till twelve o'clock at night,—for
the patriotic purpose, I suppose, of providing at
once a useful light for the footsteps of the
passengers through our evening streets, and a
pleasing delassement for their optics : not to mention the advantages which these attractive exhibi-
tions offer to the interests of another very numerous
class of traders, whose primitive notions induce
them to carry on their operations in the open air :
I dare say as many pockets have been picked outside the lighted shops of London, as inside them.

There is also another highly useful and agreeable result of this practice. I mean the keeping
at home till bed-time innumerable nuisances—
parallels to the critical *calicots* of Paris—who
would otherwise infest our minor theatres, and
give a too classical tone to their performances :

for there is no one so fastidious in his tastes as your fashionable shop-man.

But to the plot itself,—for with *this* anticipated effect of it, I have at present little to do; though it may become a matter for serious speculation when I make you acquainted with our theatres and places of public amusement.

You are to understand, then, that it is in contemplation to call a meeting of all the London Linen-drapers, to take into consideration the propriety of shutting up their shops at what they are pleased to regard as a *reasonable* hour. As a ground for which measure it is alleged, firstly, that good housewives do not make a practice of coming out to buy linnen-drapery, long after they are gone to bed, and consequently, that the last two or three hours involve a wasteful expenditure of gas and good looks; and secondly, that linen-drapers' shop-men are *men* as well as their masters, (more shame for the said masters! they ought to be women,) and that, " as such," they should be allowed to partake in those needful recreations, both of body and mind, which the arduous nature of their occupations so obviously demand; in other words, that being employed all day long in the labour of lounging over counters, setting forth the merits of mull muslins, and expatiating on the pre-eminence of new patterns, they ought to be let loose at night to recruit their exhausted powers, both physical and intellectual, in those hospitals for invalid health and morals, the Royal Saloon, the Cyder Cellar, and the half-price pits of the Adelphi, Coburg, and Surry theatres.

I shall not venture to conjecture how far the plot in question may prove successful with reference to the above object; but this I will say, that, even if it gains all it seeks, the price paid for it will be " a penny all too dear,"—seeing that it will go nigh to cost our metropolis that one peculiar feature which distinguishes it favourably above all other great cities whatever. If an inhabitant of any other capital in the world, great or small, were to be driven through the principal streets of London for the first time, at nine o'clock at night, even in the depth of winter, he would enquire what grand fête was going on ; and when you told him this was the every night aspect of the place, he would give you credit, or perchance *dis*credit, for practising upon him that only form of joke with which he thinks we solemn English are acquainted—namely, the hoax.

And this sole redeeming peculiarity in the internal economy of our Capital, we are to be deprived of at one blow—this single " Gaiety " in our

huge volume of metropolitan " Gravities" we are
to see cut out before our faces—in order that certain slim apprentices and simpering shop-men
may have time to sip their tea at sixpenny coffee-
shops, and then proceed to recreate themselves
after the intellectual labours of the day, by uttering enlightened critiques on the merits of the last
new monkey-piece at the Surry, or espousing the
cause of some victim of managerial tyranny at the
Tottenham Court Road, or pronouncing profound
untruisms on the delicate distinctions which exist
between the *tragedy* of Mr. Huntly and Mr. Cob-
ham at the Coburg !

The truth is, I suspect that the managers of
these major of the minors are the bottom of this
worse than gunpowder plot; and as there is no
knowing what their influence may bring about,
when aided by all the eloquence of all the junior
Waithmans, (who are said to be at the top of it,)
I have determined to lose no time in chaperoning
you through the gas-lighted streets of London,
while we can still find something in them to distinguish one from another : for pleasant as they
are when their shops are opened, and give to each
of them a distinct and noticeable character,—when
they are shut up, their total want of architectural

merit makes it merely like walking through interminable lines of gas-lighted brick-kilns.

We will, if you please, commence our perambu-
lation at a point which it is the more necessary
you should see now in imagination, inasmuch as
it is one which, I suspect, your somewhat exclusive notions touching the limits of visitable localities will lead you to avoid when you come among
us.   Lady M——h alleges,——as an excuse for not
visiting her stately friend, the M——ue, who dares
to live in Bedford Square,——that nothing can prevail upon her horses to pass to the north of Oxford
Street.   And I'm inclined to think *your* horses
will very soon acquire a similar distaste towards
certain quarters.   This at least I am sure of, that
two or three of the families with whom you will
be most intimate, will do their possible to persuade you of the absolute impracticability of Ludgate Hill, beyond that precise point occupied by
the far-famed emporium of Messrs Rundell and
Bridge, and will assure you that no instance ever
came within their experience of any *known* person having penetrated farther.

The spot from whence we are to start, on our
evening tour in search of the London picturesque,
shall be that where the Poultry abuts upon Corn-

hill; for even I, who am by no means fastidious as to the particular latitude in which I let myself be seen, will not pretend to have penetrated farther towards the East Pole than the immediate purlieus of this point, where the Prince of the City gives his annual dinners. Not but I believe the passage to be practicable ; and indeed I have some thoughts of exploring it myself, as far as certain points which have been discovered by Grimm's Ghost, (of course you read the New Monthly,) and by him denominated Crutched Friars and Saint Mary Axe. And if I do so, I shall certainly imitate the example of our equally adventurous northern explorers, and affix new names to certain noticeable spots. Indeed, I do not know that I can do better than adopt the identical ones chosen by those modern Columbuses. If not quite so flattering, they will be to the full as appropriate. What, for instance, can be better than to call the little narrow defile which flanks the great monument and mausoleum of our national wealth, the Bank, *Baring's* Straits ; that spot about the 'Change where innumerable apple-women congregate, *Burrow's* Point ; and that other, where the losing gamesters of the Alley first issue forth to utter their angry bewailings, *Croaker's* Sound ? But this, by the bye.

You are to understand, then, that we begin our walk at the Mansion House;—turning our eyes eastward before we set off, and casting up a glance, first, on our right, at that gloomy monument of city grandeur, which has been smoked till it looks as black upon all around it as the pots in its own far-famed kitchen; but is, nevertheless, not without a certain air of dingy dignity, which would be less exceptionable than it is, if the building were not perched up above its natural position, by means of certain mysterious arches, which run beneath it like the vaults of a church, and the darkness of which is made visible, all day long even, by a single sepulchral lamp hanging at the extreme end.

In a line with the face of this really fine building runs that principal vein in the mine of our London wealth, Lombard Street: so denominated, in courtesy, I suppose, to Sir William Curtis; that most lumbering of all the Lombards:—for anywhere else it would be called a lane. It is, in fact, at present, not wide enough to admit two ordinary aldermen abreast; and I understand that Sir William himself has it in serious contemplation to move next Session for leave to bring in a bill for widening it; as he alleges that at present he cannot pass up it, in his way to his banking house of a morning, without the eminent danger of crushing some of his own clerks against the walls.   I am told, too, that considering the buildings of Lombard Street are of *brick*, and not of *wood*, he intends to throw out a hint, for the better judgment of the House, as to whether it might not be an improvement on the usual method, if they were to grant him leave to bring in a *pickaxe* instead of a *bill*.

The other creeks that pour their ever-running streams westward at this point, and form a confluence into the rapid river of Cheapside, are, to the left of Lombard Street, Cornhill, the resort of Lucky Lottery office keepers, Stationers, and Stage-coaches ;—to the left of that, the space behind Bank Buildings, which is used chiefly by Mr. Soane, as a sort of public exhibition-room for the display of his taste in manufacturing pillars of that particular order which are intended to support only themselves, and have capitals that are anything but capital ;—and finally, to the left of this, with the chef-d'œuvre of the above-named tomb-builder between, is the little street, or rather strait, which I have alluded to before, and which has an unaccountable air of melancholy about it, that even the endless jokes of the endless Paddington-stage-coachmen who have lately been quartered upon it, are unable to dispel.

The whole of this purlieu, on which, in virtue of
our politeness, we are now about so unpolitely to
turn our backs, would, unless I am greatly misin-
formed by a city friend who is not ashamed to
own a familiarity with it, afford food for a very
instructive epistle; and it is by no means impossible
that I may hereafter fulfil my already-hinted-at
intention of exploring it with this view.   But at
present we must follow the example of the love-
sick lady in Burns's song, and " keep looking to
the west" all the rest of the evening; especially
as it is only by day-light, and at a particular hour,
that the district we are leaving behind us can be
seen to proper disadvantage.

If we shall, in the course of our evening pilgri-
mage, pass through several scenes more striking
than this of Cheapside, or more picturesque from
their scite and style of building, or more brilliant
from the boundless expense bestowed on the embellishment of particular portions of them,—we
shall meet with none that is upon the whole so
gay, spirit-stirring, and full to overflowing of
variety and life.   In almost all the principal
streets except Cheapside, if we meet with here and
there a shop whose splendours put to shame even
its splendid neighbours, we shall also meet with
here and there one whose comparative poverty

makes us wonder how it can possibly afford to keep such company. But in Cheapside there is no such disagreeable dissimilarity. Each seems determined to shine equally with its neighbours, and none is ambitious of *out*-shining them.

In fact, the housewives east of the Mansion House repair to Cheapside, as to a sort of general mart for whatever they may want under ordinary circumstances,—without determining beforehand at what particular shop they intend to make their purchase. Whereas, the inhabitants of all other districts of the metropolis go direct to so-and-so house, or to such-a-one's shop; and they find themselves on Ludgate Hill, or in Piccadilly, or Oxford Street, because the favourite emporium happens to be situated there.

Which practice is the wiser of the two, is a mystery into which it is not my present pleasure to penetrate. It is quite sufficient for me that the former has made Cheapside the most lively, various, and amusing street in all London, taking length for length; unless, indeed, you should say that I am putting the effect for the cause, and that it is the street which has made the practice, not the practice the street. This point I promise to argue with you when we meet, and to prove, to the entire dis-satisfaction of each of you, that you are each wrong, whichever side of the argument you may espouse.   In the mean time, let us proceed in our walk; or rather let us begin it;—for to my want of shame be it spoken—(and I fear to the sad discomfiture of the worthy governor's patience,) I have not yet led you a single step on your way.   ·

Passing on, then, to the western extremity of Cornhill, where Cheapside nominally begins, we shall find that the coup-d'œil of this latter is by no means striking, even now by gas-light; for though it is brighter than almost any other part of London, the private lights are so intermixed with the public ones, that all regularity of appearance is destroyed, and with it all istinct and uniform effect. Not but what the converging lines of parish gas, with the fourfold one which terminates them in the centre of the street, may easily be traced by an eye practised in this terrestrial astronomy; just as an accomplished star-gazer can trace the constellations amidst the seeming confusion of the heavens.   The light from the shops, too, at this early hour, when they are all open, eclipses all the *diffused* light of the lamps, and you see them by their form merely,—just as you see the planets and other larger stars, when there is a bright moon in the sky. This uniform confusion of lights is also scarcely at all varied, as it is in most other streets, by remarkably conspicuous points, on which the eye is as it were compelled to rest, whether it will or no. It is not the fashion here, as it is elsewhere, to insist on being known as the proprietor of a lamp as big as a light-house.

Neither can I, as before hinted, introduce you to many very conspicuous shops in this street, either for the surpassing splendour of their embellishments, or the richness of their wares. There is one, however, which cannot be passed by without notice; since it is perhaps the handsomest house of retail business in all London. This is Mr. Tegg's new emporium for everything connected with writing and reading,—from the New London Encyclopædia of all Sciences, Arts, and Knowledge, down to the sixpenny bottle of ink, the penny-worth of wafers, and the ream of " outsides," by the aid of which the forthcoming number of it will in all probability be put together.

There is a *keeping* in the character of Mr. Tegg's shop, which I admire in all things. It is as interminable as some of the new-old works which he has begun to issue from it " in numbers"—and the above-named more than any perhaps : like that, you cannot see to the end of it.   It is however a noble place ; and the outside of it is worthy the in— being of richly carved stone from top to bottom, and built (and I believe it was inhabited) by Sir Christopher Wren.

Extremes meet, in more senses than we are apt to believe, or willing to admit.   Perhaps if it were asked, at any given time, which of all the merely thriving, but still unnoticed and unknown inhabitants of any given city or district, is most likely to outstrip all his competitors, and reach to the head of his class, the prophet who pitched upon the poorest and least externally promising, would be nearest to the truth of the event.   Mr. H— of Sydney's Alley, is beyond comparison the richest shopkeeper in all London ; and they tell me it was but the other day (some twenty years ago) that he kept a six-penny stick shop on the very spot where he has since contrived to accumulate a mine of wealth. And Mr. Tegg, whose splended emporium has just gained him the honour of an introduction to your acquaintance, I myself remember, only two or three years ago, as the master of a little shop over the way, the back part of which (a sort of cabin about six feet square, which, from its heat and crowd during its hours of business, might have been inaptly enough termed the black hole

of Cheapside) he used to devote to the purposes
of an evening mock auction, for the sale of cheap
editions of popular works, to stray apprentices
" of a literary turn," who happened to be passing
by on their errands ; while his lady was selling
the same works in the front shop, for fifty per
cent. more, or less, according to the more or less
sanguine temperament of the body of bidders
who happened to be collected behind. So much
for philosophy and scandal. Now to our walk
again.

On reaching the western extremity of Cheapside we shall of course deploy to the left a little,—
leaving the endless, and as it should seem, eternal
scaffoldings of the (intended) New Post Office on
our right, and not even condescending to cast a
single glance down the dreary defile of Pater-
noster Row,—that dark domain of the Booksellers,
from which issue forth (like the Winds from the
black cave of Eolus) those winged messengers of
the national mind which make their way to the four
quarters of the Globe.

Saint Paul's Church Yard, upon which we
emerge immediately on quitting Cheapside, undoubtedly bears away the bell, in point of liveliness, from all other existing burying-grounds—
not excepting that of Père la Chaise itself, at

Q

Paris. At least such is the case with respect to the northern side of it, along which we are now to pass. As for the opposite side, *that* bears exactly the same resemblance to its gay counterpart, as the dead half of the Lady of Fashion does to the living one, in that edifying print which, when I was a boy, (you smile, as if you thought me one still!) used to attract such solemn attention from

> " The white upturned eyes,
> Of wondering mortals that fell back to gaze on it,"

as it hung against the centre pane of Mr. Bowles's print shop farther on.

Let us, however, not pass a step forward on our way, till we have looked up at the Cathedral, which here rises before us, like the shadow of some great mountain.

To use the favourite phrase of a certain assembly when the orator who is " in possession of the house" is about to advance what he feels to be a very questionable proposition,—" I have no hesitation in saying" that St. Paul's Cathedral can never be seen to so much advantage, in point of general effect, as at this time of the evening, when it cannot be seen at all! In the day time we can see just enough of this unrivalled temple—for you may take my word that it *is* unrivalled, even by Saint Peter's at Rome—to discover that it might just as well *be* at Rome, keeping Saint Peter's company, for any general impression that we can receive from it as a whole,—in consequence of the horrible manner in which the houses are crowded around it, almost up to its very doors on every side. In fact, whatever the worthy governor may hint to the contrary, I am not starting an idle paradox, but stating a simple truth, when I say, that by day-light Saint Paul's is invisible. It is physically impossible to see it—just as much as if it were out of sight;—because, to see any given object, the laws of optics absolutely require that the eye should be placed at such a distance as will permit the rays of light to enter it from every point of the outline; and this distance, in the case of Saint Paul's, is at least twenty times as great as any at which you can place yourself. Consequently, you can no more see Saint Paul's when you are walking in Saint Paul's Church Yard, than you can see Mont Blanc when you are climbing up the side of it. But now, when the whole air immediately about you is in a blaze of light, from the gas and the shops, you do better than *see*, you *feel* it; for, as the effect of the lights reaches to a comparatively small distance they do not in the

Q 2

least degree illumine the building, but only make
it show more black by the contrast: so that it
seems to stand lowering down upon you, like one
of the enormous living shadows in Milton, or

" Like Demogorgon, a tremendous *gloom*."

Saint Paul's Church Yard is to the city what
the Burlington Arcade, which we shall visit by
and by, is to the West-End—a sort of mart for
fancy matters, when the good citizens have a
mind to be more than ordinarily generous, and
pay more for a thing than they think it's worth.
This is the greatest thoroughfare for pedestrians
in all the city; as it collects all that are going
westward, from both sides of Cheapside. The
consequence of this is, that the shops pay higher
rents than anywhere else; and the consequence of
this is, that they ask higher prices and profits;
and the consequence of *this* is, that, in order to
get them, they make a smarter external shew than
they otherwise need do; and the consequence of
this is, that they attend more to what their wares
look than what they *are* ; and the consequence of
this is, that Saint Paul's Church Yard is, without
exception, the prettiest place in all the city in
which to spend money that you don't know what
to do with upon things that you don't want.
You are to understand, too, that Saint Paul's

Church Yard is a spot belonging exclusively to the City,—the very circumstance which makes its fortune with the inhabitants of *that*, (namely, its being no thoroughfare for carriages), altogether precluding it from the patronage of any but pedestrian purchasers. As it cannot boast any shops claiming particular mention to the disparagement of their fellows, we will pass on to Ludgate Hill.

On reaching the top of Ludgate Hill, we stand on a spot which will not be absolutely interdicted, to the lady part of the circle for whose edification these epistles are indited ; for those persons who set the fashions are not such fools as those who cannot afford to follow them would insinuate ; but, on the contrary, know when they are well served better than their inferiors. It does not follow, from this, that a good shop shall be a fashionable one ; but it does follow that a fashionable one is invariably a good one, and at least as cheap as a hundred worse. Now Ludgate Hill can boast three or four shops that are fashionable, even among fashionable people ; so that it must not be treated as a place absolutely unknown even in the western world. I believe Mr. Everington's show of India shawls really is matchless, notwithstanding his advertisements declare as much. Ellis's depôt for " everything in the world" of Haberdashery is unrivalled, for united cheapness and goodness. And all the first-rate jewellers and silversmiths in London inhabit Ludgate Hill, and have done for this hundred years past, in the single establishment of Messrs. Rundell and Bridge.

For a street which is gifted with two sides of the way, (and there are very few of the principal ones in this enviable predicament), Ludgate Hill is the most popular and populous in all London. At whatever time you visit it—morning, noon, night, and all night long—it is everywhere alive with busy faces, and its houses are shaking to their very foundations with the rattle of innumerable wheels. But at the time we are passing down it—just at night-fall, when the lamps are lighted, and the shops are none of them shut—it is more bright and busy than any other, or than itself at any other time. It is, however, a street of business merely, and nobody ever sets foot in it that can keep away : which I think shews a singular want of taste : for those who cannot find an hour's amusement in the mere shops of Ludgate Hill, will look in vain for it elsewhere.

The view from the upper end is not striking; for the street takes a bend about half way down; and though brilliantly lighted with public lamps, the private ones so intermix with them, that all regula-

rity is destroyed. But in detail Ludgate Hill more
than makes up for its deficiencies of general effect.
The shops are all good without exception; which
is not true of any of the streets farther westward.
And some of them are unrivalled. There is nothing in London equal to Ėverington's India ware-
house—nowhere else so much expence incurred,
with so little mere empty display of it. The two
great arched windows, each consisting of only
four immense plates of glass held together by
almost invisible polished brass frames, introduce
the eye to vistas which seem almost interminable,
from the ever multiplying mirrors with which the
whole interior of the shop is lined. The principal
lights, too, are so placed, in the centre of each
window, that they shall break the vacancy without destroying the extent of the view. They consist of several gas-burners, placed in a sort of
Chinese pagoda or temple, composed of richly cut
glass; without any brass or other ornaments to
take off the lightness and brilliancy of the effect.
These are placed over the counter in the centre of
each window; and there is another depending
from the ceiling, in the centre of the shop: so
that, when lighted, the place is tenfold more
brilliant than during the brightest sunshine. The
floor is covered with rich Brussells carpetting;

every part of the walls, from floor to ceiling, and the whole of the ceiling itself is entirely covered with looking-glass ; and the articles placed in the windows are so few, and are hung in such drapery-like fashion, that, aided by the great Indian jars which are generally displayed among them, the whole looks, from without, like a splendid drawing-room lighted up for a party, or a fairy scene in an oriental melo-drama.

To this general approval, however, of Mr. Everington's taste, I must put in one exception, in justice to my own. I do not object to his employing a plate-glass multiplication-table for the purpose of increasing, *ad infinitum*, his shawls and his shopmen ; but I cannot approve of that part of the arrangement which prevents his fair customers from judging whether the latter stand upon their heads or their heels.

There are three or four other shops in the same trade, close to the above on either side, that do their best to rival the one which first set them an example of expensive embellishment. But though they display as much light, and ten times more gilding, they fall short of their rival in tasty richness of effect. They, however, surpass it in the variety and beauty of the objects they offer to the mere passing eye—the other merely *indicating* its

calling, by the display of a few elegant nonde-
scripts in the shape of shawls.

I wish *this* had been your season for coming
among us ; and as you would never guess the reason *why* I wish so, I must tell you ;—it is this,—that
you will never have such another opportunity of admiring the genius (for they have displayed nothing
less) of our English pattern-drawers. The windows of the linen-draper's shops have this season
been at least as well worth looking at, for the
" works of art" they have displayed, as the R. A.'s
exhibition was.

I'm not joking, I assure you, nor even exag-
gerating, according to my own feelings of the
matter. I do not think anything so beautiful in
its way was ever before invented, as the patterns
of the morning dresses of this season have been :
and I pique myself on being something of a con-
noisseur in these matters. The prevailing trait of
them has been, brilliance and variety of colours—
chiefly the primitive, or rainbow colours—and
often all these united in one pattern. But the
effect produced in many cases has been what I
could not have thought possible—a species of optical illusion, produced by printing one pattern
over another, and sometimes two—so as to give
the impression of seeing one through the other.

But if these beautiful things have not yet penetrated to your remote regions, you must e'en suspend any notion you wish to form of them till they do; 'for one of their chief merits is that they must ever remain nondescript.

In the mean time, let me offer your imagination my arm, and let us proceed towards Fleet Street; for I feel that I am keeping you a most unconscionable time here in the very heart of the city. But as you will probably never condescend to visit that spot in any other vehicle than the present, perhaps you will forgive me.   We must, however, not quit Ludgate Hill, (the Bond Street of the city,) without observing that what was lately its most distinguishing feature, is now undergoing a change which I cannot but think is anything but an appropriate one; though I expect few will agree with me in this opinion. You must know that Rundell and Bridge (you have heard of *them*, I suppose, even in Yorkshire) have hitherto seemed to pride themselves on owning the most ugly, old-fashioned, and ill-conditioned domicile in all the city—so far as external appearance goes.   And for my part, I always used to think there was something high in this—that it indicated a fine, bold-faced plebæanism, to make all the Nobles of the land, up to

Royalty itself, after passing through the purgatory
of the Strand and Fleet Street to arrive at their
emporium, find the entrance to it less gainly—
less prepared and adorned for their reception—
than that of the trunk-maker higher up, or the
tin-shop lower down,—which were never destined
to be entered by any personages more exalted in
rank than a stockbroker's valet, or an alderman's
housekeeper. To make " the nobility and gentry"
come into the City at all, was bad, or rather good
enough, I used to think ; but to see their splendid
equipages—a dozen or a score at a time—standing
about the door of the shabbiest looking shop in it—
was better. It seemed as much as to say, you need
us, more than we need you, and we'll let you
know it. But besides this purse-proud display of
a London citizen's amour-propre, I used to think
there was something characteristic and appropriate in the entrance to these modern mines of
Galconda being, like the entrance to all other
mines, dark, gloomy, and forbidding ; to say
nothing of its affording a politic contrast to the
blaze of splendour which greets you on getting
within.

But alas ! all my profound speculations on this
matter were the other day, as I was passing by,
buried in a moment, beneath a shower of bricks

and mortar that came tumbling down about the ears of my friends the two golden salmon that used to stand sentries over the old-fashioned door-way, and that I can remember as a sort of city land-mark as long as I can remember the City itself. And I have now been obliged to come to the sorry conclusion, that avarice was the only ambition of these modern Crœsuses, and that it was not till each partner in the firm could reckon his wealth by millions, that they would permit themselves to be seduced, by the examples of their neighbours and the warnings of their surveyor, into the heart-and-purse-rending extravagance of laying out a few thousands merely to accommodate their cus-tomers, and without having anything more sterling to show for it than bricks and mortar.

That *this* was the feeling which preserved the old entrance so long, and *not* the one which I had foolishly enough fancied, is clear; for now that they have made up their minds to demolish it, in-stead of supplying its place by a plain, unpretend-ing, old-fashioned erection, such as my *first* theory would have required, they have run up the most " *high*-fantastical " affair in all the town, and one that, for a certain tasty want of taste, is not to be surpassed even in Regent Street itself.

On passing from Ludgate Hill to Fleet Street,—

which is a continuation of it on a gentle rise to the west, as the former is to the east,—we traverse the north end of Bridge Street, which is terminated at the opposite end by Blackfriars Bridge. This is the best street in the City, and has less than any, that perfectly *city* air which belongs to all the others. It is the Pall Mall of the City; consisting, like that, chiefly of private houses—private in appearance, but most of them used for purposes of trade. We will not pass down it, but merely glance at the double converging line of brilliant lamps, uniting at the end with the ascending, and then descending arch of them which is formed by the rise and fall of the Bridge.

The execrable line of sheds which face the end of this street,—continuing in the same line all the way to Holborn, and called Fleet Market,—we will *not* glance at; because they would disgrace the Capital of the Caribbee Indians,—not to mention the Capital of the World.

Before quitting this spot, let me say that there is no other so well adapted for observing that finest and most characteristic among all our metropolitan phenomena, a genuine London Fog. To stand opposite the Obelisk at the head of Bridge Street, when one of these far-famed fogs is coming on, and look eastward up Ludgate Hill to Saint

Paul's,—which is perhaps just distinguishable in the distance, like a deeper shadow seen through a less deep one;—westward, up the winding defile of Fleet Street;—southward, along Bridge Street, where the thickening mass comes rolling up from the Thames, cloud over cloud, each gleaming with the light of the gas;—and northward, down the long line of demoniacal looking dens of Fleet Market, where the flaring oil lamps of the stall keepers seem to struggle with the overwhelming gloom;—this, I say, is a sight worth coming all the way from Yorkshire to see, and very likely to drive you all the way back again when seen.

Fleet Street and the Strand form, for a strait street, the most crooked one we have. It runs a mile due east and west, and yet at no one point does it present a coup-d'œil worth standing still to dwell upon. They manage these things better everywhere else, it must be confessed. True, few other cities can boast of such a street as this. But those which have one contrive to make the most of it; while we, somehow or other, seem to set our wits to work to make the very least of it. Here is, for its length, the most busy, populous, and lively street in the world, perhaps. And yet you can make nothing whatever of it as a single thing —can get no great and general effect from any portion of it ; but are compelled to examine it, if at all, in mere detail, as a whole parcel of short streets, strung together as if by accident. Its best quality is its infinite variety. Being the only direct passage from the West End of the town to the City, it is the most populous thoroughfare of London. Consequently, it is the favourite resort of adventurers in every class of trade, in distinction from those who have already established themselves, or whose particular calling does not depend on mere chance patronage. It is the favourite spot for the coup-d'essai of young beginners, who fancy that nothing is to be done except in the midst of a perpetual noise and bustle. But they soon find it the Purgatory in which they are destined to remain, to qualify themselves for those Elysian fields of all London shopkeepers, Bond Street and Regent Street.

The consequence of all this is, that the whole of Fleet Street and the Strand does not contain a single *favourite* shop. In all my shopping chaperonings, I do not remember to have leant against the door-post, or stood with my back to the fire-place, or sat half on half off that anomaly in household furniture, the shop-chair, of a single house in this whole line of street. In short, it is altogether *ungenteel* to buy anything in Fleet Street

or the Strand, and nobody does it but those two
numerous classes of persons, who know no better,
and who cannot help themselves,—including in the
former class Country Cousins from the eastern coun-
ties, who are determined to get far enough westward,
even if it costs them a lodging in Norfolk Street;
and in the latter class all those improvident persons who purchase what they want, not when
they want it, but when they happen to see it
before their eyes; and as this is likely to happen
oftener in *this* line of street than in any other, it
is *here* that they oftenest buy. In fact, the shop-
keepers of Fleet Street and the Strand depend
entirely on chance; and I dare say few of them
expect, and not many of them wish, ever to see a
customer a second time.

As the constant life and bustle of this line
of street, and its ceaseless din of coaches and
carts, require an exclusively metropolitan taste to
appreciate them, I shall take it for granted that
they will present no great attractions to *you*, and
shall therefore not detain you much longer in the
midst of them; merely pointing out a few of the
noticeable spots as we pass quickly along. . And
first let me place you before the new opening a
little way up on the left, in Fleet Street, which
has lately been made by a great fire.

The rage for *improvement* in the present day has amounted to a pitch nothing short of romantic; for it has actually impelled the citizens of London, in Common Council assembled, to lay their heads and purses together for the purpose of sacrificing some fifty feet of the frontage of Fleet Street, in order to gain—what, do you suppose?—a shorter cut to the 'Change? or a grand opening to some new Bazaar? or an imposing approach to some "eminent" Assurance office? No—nothing of all this, nor nothing like it; but merely a view of the handsome spire of St. Bride's Church!

Oh! that some patriotic incendiary, now that the good citizens are in the humour for taking advantage of happy accidents of this nature, would contrive to set fire to both sides of St. Paul's Church Yard, and burn to the ground every thing it contains, outside the railing—not excepting the new front of St. Paul's School! We should then have some chance of seeing for ourselves, and showing to others, what would, if we *could* see and show it, be the boast of our island, but is now little better than its disgrace,—since we are content to sacrifice it to a few paltry shops. I suppose there never was such a blunder committed, by a people that pretends to know the value of money, as to lay out several millions of

R

it upon a building which is professedly erected
purely to be looked at, but which nobody can see
any more than if it were not there.   Truly, the
English are *not* " the most thinking people in the
world," after all.

But we are wandering and standing still at the
same time.   Let us pass on,—merely observing,
that from the commencement of Fleet Street may
be best seen, in both directions, that fine and pe-
culiarly characteristic effect which is never absent
from our evening streets in this part of the town.
I mean the gradually immersing of the farther end
of every vista into that dun, dusky distance—that
" palpable obscure"—which is infinitely more appropriate to a great city than the airy lightsome-
ness which some of them so foolishly affect.   In
moving along through the principal streets of the
city part of London, on a thoroughly dark December evening, you can scarcely help fancying yourself traversing the illuminated galleries of a vast
Mine, or of some city built *beneath* another city.
And this is just as it should be.

There is nothing to delay us any longer in
Fleet Street; for it does not contain a single
noticeable shop, nor is there a single street branch-
ing off from it that presents the appearance of anything better than an accidental gap caused by the

separation of the walls. In fact, it is the mere pavé and trottoir of Fleet Street which constitute its merits. Just before passing out, however, through Temple Bar, we may, or rather we must observe the great lumbering clock of St. Dunstan's church, sticking out upon the end of a square beam, over the heads of Hackney-coachmen, into the middle of the street, and insisting on telling us what time it is, whether we will or no : which, in any clock but one belonging to a church, would be an impertinence.

On passing through Temple Bar, we emerge upon a scene which more than loses in characteristic effect, what it gains in openness and variety. In fact, the whole of the Strand is a sort of " debateable ground," not belonging to or partaking the character of either the city or the west end ; and I shall therefore, not detain you in it any longer than to say, that I have nothing either very pleasant or very particular to say about it. Fancy yourselves, at once therefore, at Charing Cross ; and then fancy, if you can, (which you cannot,) the fine prospect that here opens upon you on all sides.

Leaving you to enjoy this prospective prospect for a post or two, I must, as usual, break off in the centre of my subject : for I perceive, what

you I dare say perceived some-half letter ago,—
that my epistle has already reached a most unread-
able length. Adieu for a day or two.—Your loving
cousin to command,

TERENCE TEMPLETON.

THE SAME TO THE SAME.

I HAVE for a long time thought that the spot
on which I left you standing, at the close of my
last epistle, is the finest, because the most characteristic part of all London—that from which you
get the most various and extensive coup-d'œil,
and the one which is at the same time most
imbued with the spirit and genius of a *London*
view. Looking eastward, you have the gloomy
defile of the Strand, thick with smoke, thronged
and thundering with carriages of every kind, and
all alive, like the entrance of a bee-hive, with
ever-busy people passing hither and thither " as
though they would never grow *tired*."

Turning to the south, we look down what is *now*,
without exception, the finest street in London ;
that to which I would, sooner than to any one
other, direct the attention of a foreigner ;—Regent
Street, Portland Place, and Piccadilly neverthe-

less, notwithstanding. True, Parliament Street wants the flashy newness of the first of these, the imposing uniformity of the second, and the (now that the old gate is removed) literally *endless* extent of the last. But on the other hand, it has the noble width of the widest of these ; the constant bustle and traffic of the most populous ; and, mixed with some indifferent houses that serve as a contrast, several of our best and most striking public buildings—which are so arranged as to give it an air of grandeur that no other street or place in London possesses.

When buildings are, joined to each other,—as the private dwellings are, all through the rest of London, as well as the public edifices that blend with them,—of whatever character they may be individually, a want of consistency and uniformity takes away from them all unity as well as grandeur of general effect. But when they are detached, however near together, the case is entirely different. Then, each, however dissimilar from its neighbour, produces its own immediate effect on the spectator's mind, and at the same time conduces to a certain general effect which is in fact the amount of all the individual ones.

Now the public buildings in this fine street may be considered as detached ; and though, with the exception of White Hall, none of them are buildings which can, individually, excite much admiration in those who look for something more than a mere piling up of stone upon stone, yet all taken together produce a better impression than any other collection of equal extent that we can shew. Those noble private residences, too, on the left side of this street, which recede considerably, and have groves of trees and open courts before them, add to this effect in a very marked manner, by giving that comparative spaciousness the want of which so sadly destroys everything like grandeur in our metropolis. This latter effect, too, has lately been increased, by the whole pavement of this street having been Macadamized :—which phrase, being interpreted, merely signifies that the whole has been changed from *pavement* to *road ;* and that particular kind of road which, when in proper order, returns no grating, gravelly sound, but over which the carriages bowl along as if the tires of their wheels were made of felt. Nothing can be finer than the effect of this on a wide, populous, and busy thoroughfare like Parliament Street. It not only adds an apparent width to the street, but the carriages bowl over it so smoothly and silently, that the scene produces, at a little distance, the united effect of an actual scene, and of a sort of animated panorama of the same, executed on a scale " as large as life."

You are to understand, by the bye, that in the above, I am not taking you through Parliament Street, but merely bidding you look down it in imagination : for it is a street that can be seen to advantage by day-light alone ; being almost entirely without shops, and therefore with little light but that furnished by the double row of gas-lamps which sweep down its slight descent.

Looking north-westward, or to the right, from the spot on which I have placed you, the coup-d'œil is still fine, though not equal to that portion we have just turned from. It consists of irregular masses of building, separated by several wide openings, the chief of which lead away to the more fashionable parts—the real West-end of the town. As we can only see these to advantage a little farther on, we will proceed onward, through Cockspur Street.

This, like most of the other principal thoroughfares, has but one side of the way : though this has it literally ;—the other side of the road being without a continuous pathway, on account of the carriage approaches to the various splendid Club-houses which have lately been erected in this immediate purlieu ; whereas, when I say in other

instances that a street has but one side of the
way, I mean one *favourite* side, on which the
houses are worth fifty per cent more rent than on
the other.

The best thing belonging to Cockspur Street,
especially at this time in the evening, is the
prospect it gives you of the above-named Club-
houses.   They are the handsomest ornaments
the town has received since the spirit of improvement has taken possession of our rulers.
They have all the grandeur of the town residences
of our principal nobility, without any of that
gloom which always accompanies it except on
their public nights.   After dark, a nobleman's
mansion in London looks like a great tomb, except on those nights when it takes upon itself
to disturb the rest of the neighbourhood with the
rattle of wheels, from the usual time of going
to bed till that of rising again.   But these Club-
houses are transparent in every part, every evening ; and in passing by them outside, you see just
enough of their brilliantly lighted rooms, and
gorgeous furniture, to excite you to invest them
with just the sort of company that they may be
supposed to have been built for ;—for which inves-
titure, by the bye, they ought to be very much
obliged to you, seeing that, without that, they

are just so many " splendid deserts :" for an Englishman thinks he does quite enough towards an
establishment of this nature, if he subscribes his
money to it : to subscribe his *person* too, is more
than he thinks reasonable. He pays his twenty
guineas a year that he may " *belong*" to this or
that Club. But to *go* to it is considerably more
than he bargains for ; and if you insist on *that*,
you cannot do less than pay *him* !

As Pall Mall, though one of the most agreeable streets in all London, is entirely a *day* street,
and cuts but a gloomy figure at night, we will
leave it on our left, and pass up that lively anomaly, the Haymarket ;—keeping on the right hand
side of it at first, that we may have a view of
the handsome new façade of the Italian Opera,
with its lofty colonnade of iron pillars ; and continuing on the same side, that we may *not* admire
the façade of the " Little Theatre,"—because it is
neither handsome in itself, nor would it *look* so if
it really were, in the eyes of those who yearn
after the little unsightly building which it has
superseded, and in which they witnessed their
" first plays."

The Haymarket is a fine, bold-faced, open
street, which has the air of being half-devoted to
business, half to pleasure—the latter, however,

predominating. In fact, besides the two Theatres,
it is half-filled, on the western side, with taverns
and houses of public resort of one kind or
another; and it is also the first spot where you
begin to meet foreigners lounging along, with
that pleasant air of an infinite want of anything
to do, which is a virtue that no Englishman
could ever even " assume."   The Haymarket contains half a dozen French houses for the entertainment of these happy idlers; which however
seem to have been established, more with a view
to remind them of what a French Restaurant is
not, than what it is ; and to let them know what
a bad French dinner it is possible to get in London, for the price of a good English one.   The
opposite side of the way is occupied by shops,
chiefly old established ones, which have a regular
connexion belonging to them : for nobody thinks
of coming here on purpose to buy, or of buying
here by accident.   On the left of this street there
is a handsome opening, terminated by the statue
in St. James's Square; and the whole street
forms an ascent steeper than any other part of
London, except Saint James's Street, which runs
parallel with it farther west.

Since we left the Strand we have missed those
perpetual oppositely-flowing currents of human

life, which have the singular faculty, for currents,
of interpenetrating each other without being disturbed or retarded in their respective courses.
On reaching the top of the Haymarket we come
into this double current again,—which is, at this
spot, growing stronger than ever, in consequence
of its course being contracted, while its bulk is
increased by the various branches that pour it in
here, towards the east, from the Haymarket, Piccadilly, and Regent Street, and towards the west,
through the narrow straits of Sidney and Cranbourne Courts. The consequence of this confluence is, at all times of the day, and particularly
at night, that the north side of Coventry Street
is almost impassable, except to those who are
more than usually expert in the mystery of making
way under such circumstances.

The character of the shops in this street is just
what might be expected from the situation.
None of them make any conspicuous shew, because no one could stand to admire them if they
did ; and therefore most of them are such as
every neighbourhood *must* have. The only exception to this is the Watch and Snuff-box shop
of the Hawleys'—which stands just where the
current of traffic separates—and which, next to
that of the same persons in the Strand, (which I

forgot to shew you,) makes a handsomer outward display than any of its kind in London.

Just at the point above-mentioned the paths divide. We will take the left hand one, and pass into Piccadilly. This is a fine street, no doubt; and by day-light there is a character of mingled liveliness and gentility about it, which makes it the pleasantest we have, for a mere promenade. But by lamp-light it does not preserve this character; especially towards the latter half, which is lighted, or rather *not* lighted, by oil instead of gas: wherefore, those who are conversant in the parish politics of St. George's can alone tell.

The first view of Piccadilly, on entering it here, at the east end, is fine; because the gas-lights extend as far as the eye reaches, and there are few other private lights to interfere with their effect. Stepping onward a-little, we arrive at those ever-busy scenes, the Coach Offices,—ornamented by a whole menagerie of Spread Eagles, Bulls and Mouths, and Bears of all colours,

" Black, white, and grey, with all their trumpery."

These would be worth stopping at for a few moments, but that we shall meet with a still more striking specimen of the same characteristic and truly English scene, higher up. Passing these, then, we find ourselves in an open space where the buildings form a Circus, at the head of Waterloo Place on the left, and with the Regent's Quadrant sweeping away on the right. If this is not the most characteristic point of view in all London, it is without exception the most striking, and what may be called handsome—especially at night.

Waterloo Place is situated on a regular declivity, and is terminated by Carlton Palace; which building has the merit (the only one it has) of in no respect throwing into insignificance the range of which it now, in effect, forms a part. It is quite as handsome as the haberdasher's shop on the right of the street which it terminates, or the bootmaker's on the left: and it is no handsomer. Which is, I suppose, just as it should be. They say we are a Nation of Shop-keepers; and accordingly, the national architect who has immortalized himself (for at least fifty years to come) by his late improvements, seems to think that there is no reason whatever, why our Shops should not vie with our Palaces.

I think he is quite right. But then he is carrying his principle to what I am afraid some people will think an impertinent extreme. There is not a single portion of Waterloo Place, or even Regent's Street, which, taking length for length, does not put the poor Palace to open shame, even before its very face.   And as for the County Fire Office, which forms the *pendant* to the Palace, at the opposite end,——it actually looks down upon its low neighbour, with an air of infinite elevation ; and its lordly inhabitant and Director, Barber Beaumont the First, from the mode in which he directs the Morning Post to announce the Evening Levees of his Lady, evidently looks upon himself as sustaining a station at least as kingly as that of his opposite neighbour George the Fourth.

This is perhaps carrying the levelling principles of architecture rather too far.   And yet they say Mr. Nash is a great favourite even at Carlton Palace itself, which he has contrived to place in such a ridiculous predicament.   This is a singular instance of royal humility, and ought not to go without its record in the annals of the hour.

At all events, Waterloo Place is incomparably the most complete thing of the kind we possess ; and at night in particular the effect of it, seen from either end, is what I must call, for want of a better epithet, quite classical.   This effect is gained, however, at what some will consider a rather extravagant, not to say a ridiculous and contradictory expence; namely, by making a whole street full of Shops look like anything but what they *should* look like; that is to say, what they *are*. In fact, a *classical shop* is a contradiction in terms, anywhere but at Pompeii.

Turning from the view down Waterloo Place, to that which opposes it on the other side the Circus, we look upon another view which, I believe, is quite unique. The Regent's Quadrant has the merit of being still more classical in its appearance and general effect than Waterloo Place; and therefore it has the *de*merit of being still less appropriate to the purpose for which it is intended. In this gloomy climate of ours, shade is a thing that we seldom have occasion to seek, even in the country; and in London, Richard's moody question of "Who saw the sun to-day?" seldom meets with a satisfactory answer during more than two months in the year. Not that London *needs* sunshine. For my part, I think she is much better without it. She never looks so thoroughly herself as when dressed in her favourite dun-coloured cloak of sea-coal smoke. And as for "a suit of flame-coloured taffeta," it does not at all become her staid complexion and

sober deportment.   And even if she does secretly
affect finery of this kind—even if she cannot help,
now and then, in a momentary fit of spleen, complaining that the sun " disdains to shine " upon her
—the next moment she is reasonable enough to
recollect herself, and add, still with Richard,

" What's that to me, more than to *Richmond*,"

on whose ineffable beauties he looks equally
lowering ?"

But where am I getting to?   I was going to
say, that the Regent's Quadrant seems to have
been erected for the laudable purpose of shewing
that a set of shops (of which it entirely consists)
may be made to *look* even less like what they *are*,
and *be* less like what they *ought to be*, than any
part of Waterloo Place itself.   This desideratum
is obtained, in the present case, by constructing
a noble colonnade in front of the said shops ;
which, in the first place, hides them entirely from
the view of those who may be in search of them ;
and in the second place, excludes every ray of
light from them, even when they have been discovered.

But all this, you know, is the shop-keepers'
concern, not ours.   It is quite enough for us, that

the Regent's Quadrant, with its finely simple concentric colonnades of Doric pillars, sweeping round towards the left from the point where we stand, and losing themselves in each other and in the misty twilight long before they come to an end,—present one of the most effective views of this kind that any metropolis can offer.

It is lucky, however, that we are looking upon this handsome anomaly by night instead of by day; otherwise we should have to observe that the execrable English plan, of building our houses only two stories high instead of five or six, is nowhere productive of such mischievous effects, in a picturesque point of view, as in this in other respects noble range of building. When you look at the Regent's Quadrant by day-light, and as a whole, it has the appearance of being intended merely for the lower range of an erection; and you cannot help fancying how fine it will look when it comes to be completed.

The mode in which this portion of the new street is lighted produces an excellent effect; though more, I imagine, from accident than design. The range of great gas-lamps, that depend from the centre of each colonnade, give a brilliant light to the foot-path and the shops, while the

s

colonnade itself, with its massy pillars, intercepts much of the light from passing out into the carriage road, and leaves that in a state of half-shadow which is much more effective than the highest light would be.

We will now pass onward, through the spot on which we have just been dwelling, and continue our examination of this most striking part of all our metropolis ; including the range of buildings from Carlton Palace on the south, to the so much vituperated Church at the beginning of Langham Place on the north-east.   At the end of the Quadrant, Regent Street itself opens upon us in all its new-fledged beauties.   And, to be candid, I must say that I wish those who do all they can to put us out of conceit of this only noticeable achievement of our own age in the matter of architecture, would put us in the way of compassing something better, or even hint to us how such a thing *might* have been accomplished—I mean, might have been with our existing " appliances and means."   I do not want them to tell us, that if Salisbury Plain could be transplanted to the centre of London, and the Portland stone quarries could be persuaded to follow it, we might in that case build a square, a circus, a crescent, and

what not, that would laugh the low-roofed tene-
ments of Regent Street to scorn, and look down,
in all the freshness of youth, upon the spot where
the latter now stand, when that spot itself shall
know them not, except as so many heaps of pre-
mature rubbish.   But this is not the question.   I
do not want to know what might have been, if
other things had happened to be as they are not;
—but what could be, everything else being as it
was.   I do not even want to know what London
would have been by this time, if George the
Fourth had been Buonaparte, the House of Commons a Chamber of Deputies, and Messrs. Hume
and Brougham persons *in posse*.   What I desire
to know is, how Mr. Nash could have built a
better street than he has done, with the means he
had at command; and what I wonder at is, how
he has contrived to build one, half so far from
bad.

If any one of you, or all united, can solve me
these questions, do.   My paper being exhausted,
I pause for a reply; which, if I do not receive in
due course of post, I shall take it for granted
that in matters of this merely metropolitan nature
you yield the pas to my superior knowledge, and
shall in that case proceed to describe the rest of

this new, and by comparison noble, feature in the face of modern London.

In the mean time know me to be

            Your ever-loving cousin,

                 TERENCE TEMPLETON.*

   * It is proper to mention that it is not Mr. Templeton's fault if this Walk breaks off more abruptly than some of its readers may wish.   But variety being above all things else my object in the selection of these papers from the vast mass which have come into my hands, I have been fain to stop short in the middle of this and one or two other communications, the forte of whose writers is decidedly *continuation:* otherwise, I should have been forced to " curtail of their *fair proportions,*" others equally entitled to attention.—*Editor.*

BROTHER JONATHAN;

OR,

THE NEW ENGLANDERS.

BROTHER JONATHAN;

OR

THE NEW ENGLANDERS. *

REJECTED FROM THE EDINBURGH REVIEW.

If his Satanic Majesty should make up his
mind to ascend among us in the present day,

* Unless I am mis-informed, the reason this article did not appear in its proper place, is, that the writer of Brother Jonathan
has neutralized his *American* title to the patronage of the " Prince
of Critics," by becoming a writer in Blackwood's Magazine. What
still greater literary enormity (if greater there be in the eyes of
some persons) he can have committed, to have so long cut off
from critical notice one of the most extraordinary works of its
day, is more than I can guess. At all events, I am happy to
have been the medium of presenting to the public this first tolerably fair estimate of a work which (to adopt the distinction made
by its shrewd and lively critic) at least " indicates," if it does
not " display," more talent than the whole body of American literature besides.—*Editor.*†

† [Since these pages were sent to press, a paper has appeared in

it is probable his first attempt to ingratiate himself with the world will consist in writing a book.
Indeed he can scarcely do less, in compliment to
that particular school which Dr. Southey has
thought proper to do him the honour of dignify-
ing with his style and title.   At any rate, if he
should write a book, *we* shall assuredly be among
the first to " give the devil his due," whatever that
may be.   Let us then not withhold it from a
person almost as little likely to think, act, or
write like other people.

It is said that when a certain distinguished secre-
tary of the present day first turned his back (not
" upon himself," but) upon his native country, Ireland, and came up to seek his fortune in the great
world of London, he was introduced to Cumberland ;
and that the literary veteran exclaimed when he was
gone, " a talking potatoe, by G—d !"   And on this
our first interview with the author before us, sober-
suited critics as we are, and therefore altogether
unaddicted   to   the   style   exclamatory,   we   can

the London Magazine, the anonymous writer of which claims the
authorship of Brother Jonathan.   And truly the paper writer,
whoever he may be, is, in some respects, not an unlikely person
to have produced the novel.   But there is no saying : for if the
writer in the magazine is to be believed on his word, there's no
believing a word he says.—*Editor*.]

scarcely refrain from uttering aloud, " a writing savage, by G—d !"—for that the work, the title of which we have placed at the head of this paper, *is* the production of a North American savage, we have no doubt whatever ; and if our " exquisite reason " for so thinking be demanded of us, all we can give is, that it *can* be the production of no one else.

Not to stand shilly shally over it, (which is a mode of treatment it will bear less than any other,) Brother Jonathan is, we will venture to say, the most extraordinary work of its kind which this age of extraordinary works has put forth—in Great Britain, we mean : what America or Germany may have produced in this sort, is more than we are able to say ; and the former of those countries in particular, may, for any thing we know to the contrary, be able to count a whole catalogue of similar works, written by the same hand — or rather hands—for we imagine this person employs *both* his hands at the same time, one on one volume, and the other on the another ! At least, we can at the moment hit upon no other theory, to explain the extraordinary and headlong rapidity of style, as well as the insane incoherence of matter, which prevail throughout these volumes—

which "*prevail*" throughout them, but which (be it expressly understood) are far from being their only distinguishing characteristics, and which are still less the causes of our feeling called upon to notice them.

In fact, the author of these volumes, whoever he may be—whether " a saint, a savage, or a sage," and whether this be his first work or his fiftieth, (and it *may*, from its internal evidence, be either the one or the other,)—is, to say the least of him, the most *original* writer of his day; and we are greatly mistaken indeed, if he will not turn out to be, without one exception, the most extraordinarily gifted of them all, as far as mere natural faculties go.   How   far adventitious circumstances   may   interfere,   to   frustrate   the operation of those faculties, or turn their effects to evil account instead of good, is more than we shall pretend to predict, in the present early stage of our acquaintance with their possessor ; but that *no* circumstances can ever *neutralize* them, we are confident.

Brother Jonathan, if it must be classed at all, may be placed under the head of that altogether modern anomaly, the historical novel ; and if an express object must be assigned to it, it will be that of illustrating the manners of the Americans, and of the New Englanders in particular, at the commencement of the American Revolutionary War. And in fact, the work *does* furnish this illustration, in a most striking and effective manner; and as no other work does, and no other writer that we are acquainted with is at all likely to do. But the truth is, that neither the above, nor anything else, can be assigned as the specific object and end of this singular production,—which we conceive to have been written, not as a means to any end whatever, but as an end in itself.

We live in an age when, for the first time in the history of mankind, authors may be said to be *natural* productions: that is to say, they spring up necessarily, out of the circumstances of the times. We imagine that the writer of Brother Jonathan was *born* an author, and that he could no more have failed to fulfil his calling, than he could to have exercised any other of the active functions of his nature. His mind is of such a character and constitution, that it could not choose but fill itself to overflowing with ideas and images, no matter by what circumstances it might have been surrounded; and being so filled, it cannot choose but pour its contents forth, like an overflowing vessel,—

reckless of all consequences, and without any necessary reference to recipients.   If he were thrown
upon a desert island to-morrow, and left without
the remotest hope of escape from it, he would, the
day after, begin writing at the rate of fifty pages
a-day, and never cease till his materials were exhausted : we mean his *material* ones ; for his moral
ones would never be likely to fail.   The former
deficiency being, under present circumstances, not
within hope, we see no probable end whatever
to the productions of his pen.   At any rate, Dr.
Southey may abandon his reported project of
achieving immortality by writing more than Voltaire did ; for here is a person, who, if he lives
to the ordinary age of man, may, if he pleases,
write more than all that Voltaire *has* written, and
all that Dr. Southey *intends* to write ; and it will
be his own fault, not Nature's, if he does not
write it all better than either !

The reader will be able to form some faint notion of the fertility (for we will not call it diffuse-
ness) of this writer's invention, as well as of his
pen, when we say, that though Brother Jonathan
consists of three thick volumes, of four hundred
and fifty pages each, it only manages to make us
acquainted with the events of about a year or so in

the life of its hero,—who is in fact only a boy when we are called upon to take leave of him, and who during that brief period is made to undergo as many adventures, both in love and war, as would fill the lives and furnish forth the pages of half a dozen ordinary romance heroes and romances. He has no less than three love affairs on his hands and heart, all at the same moment; each appertaining to a heroine of an absolutely distinct character; and each illustrative of a distinct kind of love. And all this takes place while he is engaged in the very thick of the " guns, drums, trumpets, blunderbuss, and thunder," of the opening of the American War.

But besides this, the hero himself, as well as every other principal character in the work, is not only him or her self, but some one, two, three, or more other persons at the same time. Add to which, we are introduced to several historical characters; two of them no less distinguished than Washington and Franklin themselves; and *one* character who, as if all this were not enough to fill up the space of one year, is gifted with the faculty of relating events that never happened at all !

We shall not attempt to make our readers ac-

quainted with the plot of Brother Jonathan ; and
if for no other reason, for this very sufficient one
—that though we have just read the work from
beginning to end, and with that undivided attention which extraordinary pleasure in the perusal of
a work always excites, we are at this present
writing as absolutely ignorant of the said plot as
if it had never been propounded to us. And to
say the truth, we consider this circumstance to be of
very little importance, where, as in the case before
us, there is enough to arrest the attention of the
reader, independently of any merely progressive
interest arising from an artificial concatenation of
events. We doubt if the Scotch Novels would be
so good as they are, if their plots were better : we
say this of them abstractedly, as works. And we
do *not* doubt, that if the writer of them had waited
to make his plots better, he would have ended
by making his works npon the whole not so good ;
for what they would gain by the process in one
way, they would more than lose in another. It is
the characters, the scenes, and the descriptions,
that we remember, and desire to remember, and
not the mere vehicle which conveys them to us,
any more than it is the paper and print which
place them before our bodily senses. And perhaps

it will be found on examination, that we feel the moral beauties of those works more during the perusal, and are better able to recall them afterwards, in proportion as the mere plots have gained little hold of our attention at the moment, and have dwelt but faintly and confusedly on the memory.

But be this as it may, the readers of Brother Jonathan will do well not to complain of its deficiencies in regard to plot : for its writer, to say nothing of his being evidently a person who will not be schooled as to what he shall or shall not write, is altogether incapable, by the constitution of his mind, even of imagining, much less of constructing, a regular concatenation of events. In short his genius is anything (we had almost said everything) but mechanical ; and we are greatly mistaken if it is not capable of producing works which shall possess every possible good quality, (not to mention every bad one,) only excepting that one (whether good or bad we shall not determine) of having a beginning, a middle, and an end.

We have said that this work is the most original of its day ; and if originality consists in a something which can be likened to no other thing that existed previously, our proposition will not be disputed by the most cavilling of critics. A work, to be perfectly original, should not merely remind us of no other work of the same class, but prevent us from thinking of any other in connection with it. And such, we will venture to say, is the case with Brother Jonathan.

But this applies generally. To be perfectly original, a work must possess characters, a turn of thought and of sentiment, and a style, altogether its own. And here again Brother Jonathan stands alone in our literature.

But then, to render its claim to originality of any value even if admitted, the materials in the management of which that originality is shewn must be drawn from the great store-house of nature, and be referable to something existing there, and therefore interesting to the mind and heart of man; otherwise the originality becomes mere eccentricity and impertinence.

And here too we are bound to say that the writer before us merits no mean degree of commendation. His characters, though they seem to come before us as if from a new world of which we had no previous notion, (as indeed so far as *we* are concerned they do,) all bear

that impress of our common nature which makes
them at once pass current with us as beings
in regard to whom we are bound to feel a human
sympathy. The thoughts and sentiments, too,
which, by a mistake common to all writers of fic-
titious narrative, he occasionally thinks fit to put
forth in his own proper person, though full
of novelty, are seldom founded in other than
sound views of the subject in question. And
above all, his style, which is more exclusively his
own than any thing else belonging to him, is so
only because he has had courage to tell his story
in the manner that is most natural to him—because he has put his heart, his memory, and his
tongue, into his pen, instead of adopting the usual
method, of letting his pen supply the place of all
these.

Let us go a little more into detail; for as we
intend to present the reader with little or no account of the plot of this work, we can the better
afford to dwell somewhat minutely upon its characteristic particulars. Conceive, then, of the
hero of a work, every event of which is fraught
with the most romantic interest, and every page of
which includes some subtle refinement of thought
or sentiment—conceive the hero of a work like

T

this, as an overgrown lout of a boy, brought up in the Back Woods of America,—with a stoop in his shoulders, a swing in his gait, hob-nailed shoes upon his feet, a smock-frock upon his back, a nasal twang in his speech, and almost every phrase he utters regular Yankee!   And conceive (if you can) how all this shall obtrude itself at every page, without for an instant weakening the interest you from the first moment feel towards this singular hero, or even throwing over him the slightest air of the ridiculous—an association which is fatal to anything like a serious interest, however deep-seated it may previously have been.

Courageous even to a pitch of mad-headed fool-hardiness,—yet occasionally trembling in his shoes with sheer affright;—open and sincere as Truth itself, —yet sometimes artful, hypocritical, and a liar;— proud and ambitious as Lucifer,—yet fooling away his time in idle fancies and effeminate dreams;— an adorer of reason and justice,—yet pursuing to the verge of destruction and death a being who never injured him ;—his heart " pure as the thought of purity,"—yet leading him to cast himself head-long (though advisedly) into the lowest depths of profligate degradation ;—high-minded and chival-rous as a hero of ancient romance,—yet heaping

daily injuries and insults on the heart that avowed-
ly adores him, and that *he* adores :---such, and a
great deal more, is the compound of contradictions
to which this author introduces us, under the
name of Walter Harwood. And yet, such is the
intuitive skill and knowledge of human nature with
which he has mixed up together (without amalga-
mating) these opposites, that in no one instance
do we feel them to be necessarily incompatible
with each other, nor do they greatly interfere with
that sentiment of deference and respect which
novel readers are bound to entertain towards a
hero of three goodly volumes.

But if the hero of this strange work is not of
the ordinary class, the heroine with which our
author has supplied him is at least a match for
him in singularity. At our first introduction
it is difficult to suppose her anything but a born
idiot. Presently, however, we begin to fancy she
is more mad than foolish, and more cunning than
either. But after a little further acquaintance
we find her one of the sweetest and purest, one of
the most delicate and feminine of all the beings
that imagination has formed from the actual
models which nature has furnished. With all
the wildness and originality, as well as all the

T 2

fervour of character possessed by her lover, she
has that equable placidity of temperament, and
that steady consistency of feeling and of purpose,
which were never allied to the former qualities
except in woman.   We know of no imaginary
character bearing the slightest resemblance to
Edith Cummin, with the exception of Mignon, in
Goëthe's Wilhelmeister—from whom it is probable
that the author before us took his notion of Edith.
But let us add, that if she wants that etherial
lightness of outline, and that thin transparency
of colouring (if we may so speak), which belong
to the singular creation of Goëthe, and which
give to it an almost spirit-like and superhuman
air, she is altogether infinitely more natural, without being either less imaginative, or less touch-
ingly simple, child-like, and innocent.   And the
consequence of this difference is, that she excites
in the reader a much more permanent and valuable, because a more purely *human* interest and
sympathy.

But as we have hinted before, our author is not
satisfied in supplying his hero with *one* heroine,
but furnishes him with no less than three; between whom he is at no little loss how to divide
himself fairly, and according to his somewhat

singular notions of right and justice in such matters. As far as *we* can judge for him, his *heart* seems to belong throughout to his first love, Edith ; his *imagination* to Olive ; and his *reason* to the poor, polluted, and spirit-broken, but pure-minded and repentant Emily.

These two latter supernumerary ladies we cannot stay to introduce formally to the reader ; but we must not pass them by without saying that both characters are drawn with great distinctness and truth, and that both evince in the author a very subtle as well as a very extensive acquaintance with the movements of the human heart ; an acquaintance, however, which we must consider as more intuitive than practical, or in other words, as springing rather from a diligent watching and questioning of his own nature, than from actual observations on that of other people.

Of the other imaginary characters introduced in this tale, we can only stay to particularize two —both of which are as entirely original as those already referred to, and both are drawn with equal vigor, spirit, and truth, so far as the extremely confused and defective nature of the plot permits us to follow and observe them. Jonathan Peters, while he retains that title, and during his appearance in the family of the hero's father, is undoubtedly sketched with a bold, masterly, and felicitous pencil. His admirable good sense, and the skill with which he applies it, in connection with his extensive knowledge of the world and the human heart, to gain and keep an overwhelming ascendancy in the family in which (nobody can tell for what reason) he has domiciliated himself at the opening of the story,—produce a most powerful effect upon the reader; an effect which is rendered necessary, in order to sustain the influence which he is afterwards to exercise (unconsciously and unintentionally) upon all the subsequent events of the story, when he has almost wholly disappeared from it. As to his after introduction, under his aliases of Warwick Savage, Evans, &c. these are among thóse gratuitous make-weights to the plot, which altogether confuse and destroy its consecutive interest, and render it little better than a wild and incoherent hubbub of scenes and incidents, producing together the effect of a feverish dream.

The other character that we have alluded to above is Harry Flemming—a sort of Ferdinand Mendez Pinto—a " liar of the first magnitude." It should seem from the principle feature of this character, as well as from some other points in the work, that our author believes in the hereditary nature of the moral qualities of man. At any rate, the only argument we are offered, to shew that Harry Flemming is the son of his father, is, that whereas the father was a little given to embellishment in his relation of any event that occurred to him, the son invents the whole story from beginning to end, and relates it in such a manner that you believe it at least as confidently as if you saw it happen. He invents too, with a sincerity of purpose, and a fervour of imagination, which almost have the effect of doing away the demerit of his delusions, by making them more of poetical creations than anything else. It has been said in accusation of poets, that they are only liars : and it may be said in excuse of our author's liar, that he is only a poet. This character does not occupy much space in the work ; but what there is of it is the most spirited sketch of the whole.

The only particular in which this singular author has chosen to follow any fashion but his own in this work, is in the introduction of other than the natural machinery of the story : whether to call it *super*, *sub*, or *un*-natural, we cannot very

well determine. In conformity with the taste of
the day, the writer of Brother Jonathan, as if his
story was not wild and incoherent enough in
itself, has made the "confusion worse confounded," by introducing a Prophet and a Witch,
who seem to act the parts respectively of good
and evil genius in regard to the hero and all his
concerns, and who contrive by their joint influence, or rather their perpetual opposition, to make
that absolutely and irremediable unintelligible,
which would have been very nearly so without
their aid. Perhaps the writer may tell us that
he has introduced these two mischievous Marplots,
because he found them in the state of society in
which his scenes are laid, and which they profess to illustrate ; and he will probably shelter
himself behind the example of our illustrious
countryman, the author of Waverley : though we
scarcely think him a person likely to plead pre-
cedent for anything he may think fit to either say
or do. The truth is, that with all his strong
sense and sturdy straitforwardness, he has a
lurking taste for the unintelligible, and a faculty
that will secure him from ever being debarred the
indulgence of it. And as to mere mystery in the
abstract, he knows very well that there cannot

be too much of that in a work which would hope
to succeed with the class of readers to whom *his*
ostensibly addresses itself; that in fact a novel,
to be popular with those who will *pay* for the
reading of it, must be " perplexed in the extreme"
—or rather, from one extreme to the other—from
the beginning to the end.

Thus far of the merely imaginative portion of
this work;—which portion, though it is undoubtedly the result of great intellectual power,
and is fraught with much scattered interest, and
every here and there with the most exquisite
touches of passion and pathos, is altogether wild,
incoherent, and unsatisfactory as a whole; and
what is still worse, it is not without a *leetle*
affectation—to adopt a New England word from
its author.

But not so the portion which is founded on
mere fact and observation. *That* is in its way,
and as far as it goes, incomparably the best illustration of American manners we have yet been
presented with. The half-savage, half-civilized
scenes at the early home of the hero, on the borders of the Back Woods—those which occur on
his journey thence to New York—those connected
with the first declaration of American indepen-

dence, and the opening of the War—the sketches
connected with the native Indian manners, and
growing out of their wild superstitions—and
finally the descriptions of local scenery—all these
are drawn by the hand not only of a master, but
of a master who has been absolutely self-taught ;
or rather, who evidently believes that there is no
teacher worth attending to in such matters, but
Observation alone ; and who therefore boldly re-
peats to us, in so many words, what she has repeated to him.

Considering the kind of scenes and the class
of manners which his narrative leads him to place
before us, it is pretty clear that such a describer
must not reckon upon the suffrages of readers
who pique themselves on the *refinement* of their
tastes.   But those who like to hear the plain
truth told in the plainest words that will tell it,
may here meet with some of the most lively,
spirited, and vigorous pictures of national manners that have ever been painted.   We have no
mincing the matter here—no squeamish keeping
out of sight of ungainly objects or obnoxious
habits of feeling—no finical fining down of
phrases—no effeminate refinements of one thing
into another, or artificial contrasts which neu-

tralize all truth of effect. In short, the author of Brother Jonathan has the wit to see, and the courage to attempt to shew, that truth and nature are quite good enough to be looked at as they really are, and are much more likely to appear *what* they really are when looked at in their nakedness, than when dressed up in the Monmouth Street foppery of falsehood and art.

We shall now present the reader with a few extracts from this singular work—without which, and indeed we are almost afraid *with* which, he will not be able to gain, from what we have said, anything like a distinctive notion of it. And to say truth, we shall not be very sorry if this should be the case, provided what we have said should lead to the general perusal of the work itself: for we are disposed to fear that the extraordinary originality displayed in Brother Jonathan is calculated to insure it anything rather than extensive popularity in the present day, unless some adventitious impulse be given to it from without in the first instance. And we are confirmed in this fear by the fact of its having been already many months before the public, without its having hitherto attracted any notice whatever.

We have already hinted at the singular cha-

racter of the heroine of this New England story.
We cannot attempt to convey a notion of Edith
Cummin by means of extracts from those portions of the work in which her character is developed.   But we will do the next best thing, by
presenting the author's conception of her.

* " Edith Cummin—we shall pass over the rest
for the present—was a Virginian ; a niece of
Abraham Harwood : a creature, so whimsical, so
contradictory, that, for many years, until her character changed, (all at once, in a single winter,) it
would have been quite impossible to describe her,
so as to give one a true notion of what she really
was ; without leading her out, making her talk,
and showing her off, in a thousand ways, at the
same time.

" She was little ; very girlish, very spirited, and
quite singular in her whole appearance ; with

---

* The reader will have the goodness to attribute the singular
punctuation of these extracts to anybody but *us*.   Whether it has
been invented by the printer of Brother Jonathan, or the author,
is more than we can guess.   But of this we have very little
doubt, that one most prevailing cause of the want of success of
the work is this very system (for it is done, not by accident, but
on a kind of system, such as it is) of pointing —which mangles
and fritters away the effect of many of the finest passages, and
changes not a few into pure and impracticable nonsense.

rich, plentiful hair, always in the way of herself, or somebody else ; a pale complexion ; large, hazel eyes, full of moonlight and water, never still for a moment :—one hour she was a woman, the next, a child, a baby, a simpleton ; with hardly wit enough to keep herself out of the fire. Now, she would be found sitting in a corner, alone ; purple with cold ; poring over some great, heavy, serious book, such as no other child, of her age, ever thought of poring over ; and, after a little time, perhaps, cuddled up in a heap, with her loose hair falling about her face ; pouting and sobbing over some poor two-penny ballad, such as no other child ever thought of sobbing over."

" She had a thousand childish ways with her ; innocent, simple ways, which there was no speaking seriously about, absurd as many of them were ; a sprightly, sincere temper ; without one atom of art, or affectation. She had a knack, too, quite her own, of bringing the water into your eyes, and a smile about your mouth, at the same time ; and always (which was the charm, after all) without intending it, or knowing it, or even caring for it, if she did know it. She loved romping ; ' *that* she did ;' and would go without her dinner any time, for a good long race with her cousin Watty's

large dog, under the elm trees; or any thing
else, for a few hearty tumbles, all alone—head
over heels—in the long fresh grass ; or the newly
mown hay, before the rich clover blossoms were
dead."

" During these pastimes, it was amusing enough
to see, with what an air, she punished all intru-
ders ; not even excepting her ' dear, *dear* cousin
Watty,' whom, in the language of old Virginia,
she loved, ' mighty bad ; so she did.'   In such
a case, at such a time, Edith would look and
speak, much more like a dwarf woman, caught
perhaps with her night-cap on, or slippers off ;
than like a sad little tom-boy, as—begging her
pardon—she certainly was.—Her large eyes would
sparkle,—so the men ' allowed '—like the mis-
chief ; and she would stand a tip-toe, with a
dignity, quite heroic, for such a diminutive little
creature.

" She was perpetually doing what nobody was
prepared for—perpetually making people jump ;
and had, if there be such a one, the faculty of
unexpectedness within her ; like a Leyden jar,
always ready to be let off.   At one time, it would
really appear, as if she had been lying in wait,
like a torpedo-fish, in the water, for an opportunity to set people tingling ; at another, as if she

enjoyed, in her very soul, the confusion of those; especially if they were grown up, who, led astray by her manner and size, had mistaken her for a child. A word, or a laugh, was enough; just when some stranger, perhaps, who had been looking at her absurd gambols, with a large dog, was on the point of pulling her into his lap, for a fine romp—only a word, or a laugh; and he would start back, as if he had been playing with an electrical machine."

" Between the upper and lower parts of her face, there was a remarkable contradiction. Judging by her forehead and look, you would call her much older; by her mouth, much younger than she was. Her large eyes were sometimes full of strange, womanly meaning; solemn and beautiful, beyond anything that we see in the eyes of children; while her mouth was always—no matter where she was—no matter though her eyes were full of tears—her mouth was always just ready for a laugh.

" Her character was like her face; whatever she did, whatever she said, was full of contradiction. She was a puzzle. She would say the strangest out-of-the-way things; now, like a little child; now, like something wiser than a woman: at one time, as if she wanted common sense; at another,

as if she were inspired.   She had, in truth, all
the simplicity of a child, with much of the woman's
loftiness."

" There wefe times also, when her thoughtful
eyes, her pale face—and mouth, like the wet rose-
bud — were brimful of something, like poetry;
and others, while she sat in the corner, with a
profusion of hair, overshadowing her whole face
—when she might have passed for an idiot; so
patiently—so stupidly tranquil, would she remain,
for a whole hour, together; looking into the
ashes, where others were parching corn; or watching the current of sparks, that rushed up the
chimney, whenever the ' back log' moved, or
the ' forestick' parted in the fire.—There was
that, also, in her look and manner, while she
was reading by herself; or listening, attentively,
to the conversation of others, which would have
been regarded, by some, as the indication of a soft
and submissive temper.   But, if anything happened; if she were taken by surprise; or found,
on looking up, that she had been observed—
there was, instantly, over all her face, a look of
insulted womanhood; a something absolutely im-
perious about her clear forehead; and a sort of
beautiful petulance about her mouth, which, before one could make up his opinion of her, would

be gone—for ever gone—like the shadow of a strange bird, from a lighted mirror." Vol. I. pp. 26–33.

Our next extract shall consist of a piece of local description, in which these volumes abound, but much of which, though steeped in a vein of fine, bold, full sounding eloquence, is rather poetical from its mistiness than picturesque from its precision and distinctness. The following, though somewhat overstrained and extravagant, conveys a gorgeous and glowing idea (not a picture) of the sight it describes.

" The autumnal beauty of a North American forest cannot be exaggerated. It is like nothing else on earth. Many a time have we gone through it; slowly tilting over a pretty blue lake, there, among the hills; our birch canoe dipping, with every motion of the paddle—the waters beneath us—all the mountains about—all—unknown to the world; in a solitude—a quiet—profound as death—and bright as heaven; the shores overhung with a superb autumnal foliage; and a sky so wonderful—so visionary—that all the clouds, and all the mountains were of a piece, in the clear water; and our boat was like a balloon.

" Say what you will, there is nothing to be compared with a scene of this kind—about an

hour before sunset—in the depth of a great North
American solitude;—a vast amphitheatre of wilderness, rock and mountain—after the trees are
changed by the frost. People may talk of their
fine Italian skies; of their hot, bright East Indian skies; of the deep midnight blue, of the
South American skies. We have seen them all;
slept under them all; slept under a sky, like one
great moon;—worshipped under them all;—seen
them through all their changes, of storm and
sunshine—darkness and light; and we say, that,
in reality, they are dim, heavy—unclouded, uninteresting—compared with your North American
skies, a little before, and after sunset.

" And so, too, of the garniture; the superb garniture of a North American wilderness, after two
or three clear, frosty nights. There is nothing
to compare with it, under heaven. The mountains—vallies—woods—all burst into flower; and
all at once. Other countries are in a better state
of cultivation. Their trees are less numerous;
their wild shrubbery, less like a vegetable inunda-
tion over the land—covering every foot of the
earth; or the changes of their colour, from season
to season, are slow and gradual.

" It is not so, in America — North America.
There, the transformation is universal—instanta-

neous. A single night will do it. In the evening of a fine day, perhaps, all the great woods will be green—with hardly a red, or a brown, or a yellow leaf. A sharp frost will set in, at night. Before the sun rises again, the boundless verdure of a whole province—a whole empire, in truth, will be changed. In the morning, there will be hardly a natural green leaf to be found. Before a week is over, go where you may, through the superb wilderness, you will meet with nothing but gay, brilliant scarlet—purple—orange; with every possible variety of brown, light blue, and vivid crimson; or blood colour. Of all the trees, none but the evergreen tribe, will keep their integrity. They will show along the battlements of the mountain—darker than ever—more cloudy than ever; like so many architectural ruins, or surviving turrets—in the splendour of the surrounding landscape.

" No, no—it is not saying too much of all this beauty — of all this great magnificence — when the fresh, cold, brisk wind of the season, gets among the branches—after such a night— and blows up the superfluous leafing, to the warm sunshine — like a tempest, among prodigious flowers—tearing and scattering the tulip coloured foliage over all the earth, and over all the

waters; *no*, it is not saying too much—merely to
say—that, under heaven—throughout all the
vegetable creation, there is no spectacle of beauty,
or show; of richness, or grandeur—to be compared with it.   Imagine—we do not mind ap-
pearing a little absurd, if, thereby, we may give
the stranger, a true idea of this appearance—
imagine, therefore, a great wilderness of poppies,
or tulips—outspreading itself on every side—
reaching quite away to the horizon—over hill, and
over valley;—or a wood, literally encumbered—
heavy—with great, gorgeous, live butterflies—for
ever in motion.

  " We have been a traveller; we have looked
upon the dark Norwegian woods—the dull ever-
greens—towering up—*into* the sky—covering
whole provinces; woods, too, of stupendous oak
—each tree, if the soil were divided, overshadowing a man's inheritance—flourishing bravely
through whole territories: more than one quiet,
solitary place—entirely shut in, by the hills—
flowering all over—all the year round.   But we
have never met with—never heard of—never
looked upon, elsewhere, that profusion of glorious
vegetable beauty, which is to be seen, every
' *fall*,' in the woods of North America; heaped
up, on all the banks of all the rivers—up—up—

to the very skies—on the great mountains—or, accumulated over the low countries—and weltering there, all the day through, in the light, or shadow—wind, or sunshine, of the season." Vol. ii. pp. 29—33.

We shall now offer a specimen of those parts of Brother Jonathan which perhaps deserve to rank as the most valuable, and will assuredly be looked upon by many as the most if not the only intelligible ones. We mean the scenes illustrative of the state of manners and society in the country where the events of the story take place. The rare merit of the following scene consists in the literal and uncompromising truth with which every part of it is given. Walter Harwood, the hero of the story, is about to leave his home in Connecticut, and seek his fortune at New York; and he is conveyed thither after the following fashion—the only one of the time.

" Walter sprang away; and came bounding over the low stone walls, and brush fences, ' like a deer,'—with a large dog at his heels. A moment more, and he was stowed away in what is called a ' stage,' in America. But Panther, somehow—the large dog—did not appear to comprehend, precisely, the nature of the arrangement. He stood still—waiting the sign from his

beloved   master — friend — companion — either   to
spring up, on the roof — into the carriage — or to
follow a-foot.

" The   driver   blew   a   farewell   blast.   Panther
moaned — but stood still.   The wheels moved —
rattled — smoked : he stood still, nevertheless,
waiting the signal, up to the very last moment,
poor fellow ; when the carriage turned out of the
lane, all at once, into the great high-road.   He
uttered a howl, when he saw that ; ran off to the
fence — rose up — and put his two fore-paws upon
the gate.   Walter saw him — heard his voice, end-
ing as he had never heard it before, in a sick,
angry, impatient yelp, or two.   He covered his
face, then ; pulled his hat over his weary eyes ;
and got back into the carriage, as far as he
could.

" ' A pooty consid'rble funny noise that, I guess
—for sich a whelp,' said one of his neighbours.
' I never heard nothin' like, it afore.'

" ' Nor I '—said another—' in all my life : ony
once—tell ye how that was, though.   One day,
our Towzle — he fit a painter ; — well — and so,
the painter, he smacks him thro' the ribs—clean
as a whistle—same as a cat ;—well ; an' so ; ever
see a cat ?—wild cat, I mean ?—well—an' so—
poor Towzle, he sets up *sich* a noise ! right away ;

jess like that ;—well—an' so, I say ; you, what's
that air dog's name ?'

" ' Poor Panther, sir—only poor Panther.'

" They had now come to another turn ; a place,
where Panther never failed his poor master, before, when he was going away. Our hero looked
out ; rubbed his eyes—glanced, hastily, over
the grounds—but no—no Panther was to be seen.
The brave brute had given up all hope. The
boy's heart sunk within him. He drew back,
further and further, into the deep seat ; with a
feeling, so unworthy of a man ; so unlike any
that he had ever known before,—through sickness
— through sorrow — that he would have wept
aloud, perhaps, if he had been altogether alone.

" ' Seems to take it ruther unkindly, judge,
hey ? '—said one of the people. " Home sick,
a few—I guess—don't you ?—wonder who that
air baby-faced gal was ; nation white, I guess—
never seed any body half so white afore ; love sick
—I guess. I say, you—sweetheart o' your'n, I
guess—hey ?'

" ' If you are speaking to me, sir,' said our boy ;
starting bolt upright ; pushing away his hat ;
and showing his lighted eyes—the brightness
whereof was rather alarming :—' If that's for me,
sir , you'd better look out.'

" ' Nation !'

" ' A leetle on the huffy order, I guess ! aint you ?—Like to have a tussel, may be ? wouldn't ye ?—or a good clever game o' rough an' tumble ?'

" ' Yes ! with all my heart—yes !—would you ? If you would, Mister, what's *your* name, you have only to say another word about my sweetheart, as you call her ;—baby-face !—ye great black lookin' lubberly beast.'

" The convulsive agitation of his mouth was quite enough. They grew still, immediately, on every side of him ; not so much from fear, as from curiosity to know more of ' sich a quair funny sort of a feller.' One gave a whistle of surprise ; another, a sort of low, good humoured growl ; after which they, and all the rest, were quiet.

" Here was the boy's first essay in outbraving ' real imperdence.' He saw the advantage of it, long before they parted ; for, all the passengers came to be on good agreeable terms with him— pleasant, free, and sociable, without being saucy."

" The ' stage' was a long, rough-built, heavy waggon ; capable of ' accommodating' twelve or fourteen people inside—they carry no outside passengers, up to this day, in that country. There was only one way of getting up to it, or into it ; and that was, over the backs of the horses, by climbing, or by storm. It would go—lumbering, pitching and jolting over the almost impassable roads, of the country, with a wheel, or two, for ever in the air—at the rate of about forty miles a-day—' more or less.'

" There were nine live passengers aboard ; with a great heap of rubbish ; and a large dead hog. Eight of the former, were human beings ; the ninth, a sucking pig. Walter, unhappily for him, was rigged out, in all his go-to-meetin' finery ; unhappily, because, he never appeared so like a great, overgrown, awkward country boy, as when he was thus equipped ; nor ever to such advantage, as in his old clothes ; a striped woollen frock—or short gaberdine ; with his collar open : —his throat naked—and his rich, loose hair huddled about his neck.

" He wore, now, a large, broad brimmed, low crowned, wool hat—newly ironed up, for the occasion—you might have seen your face in it —' a leetle o' one side '—with a flaming brass buckle, in front ; a dimity waistcoat—striped with dark yellow—it had been a petticoat of his mother's—a part of her wedding dress—the flaps hanging half down to his knees ; cow-hide shoes —newly greased with a famous preparation of the time, for keeping out water—which left a ' smooch '

upon whatever they came near ; a pair of huge
buckles in them, too ;—his hair gathered in a
club, and bound up, with a piece of sky-blue
' worsted ribbon ;' a large, bright, silver brooch,
firmly skewered into the bosom of a coarse, clean,
good-looking shirt,—which it held, as it were, by
the teeth — so that his white skin was visible
above, and below it.   His look was that of a
lubberly country boy ;—a ' jinooine ' Brother Jonathan—going forth, from his home, to ' undertake '
a school for the winter, wherein he may retail out
such learning, as he has been able to ' lay in,' at
wholesale, the summer before, at some of the
schools, academies, colleges or universities, of
North America.

"The passengers were very still, after the re-
buff, which Walter bestowed on his very curious
companion.   They were all, or the greater part of
them, nearly or quite asleep ; their heads bobbing about, all the way, as if there were no *particular* owners for them ;—all was quiet—as quiet,
in truth, as it could be, in such a carriage,
where the smothered squealing of the pig ; the
noisy rattling of the iron ware—with all the ' an'
so forths, an' so forths, and so forths,'—were
quite enough to drown the voice of an ordinary
man, while in ordinary conversation.   They got

along very well—*very*—till a sudden, rough jolt,
brought all their heads together, at once, with a
tremendous crash, on the ' near ' side of the carriage ; the other being ' up a tree '—that is—
lodged on the top of a large, rugged stump, so
that, for half a minute, or more—the ' stage '
appeared in a sort of irresolute balancing humour;
as if undetermined whether to go ' clean over,
slap'—or only part way.

" The pig squealed as if the devil was in him :
the passengers awoke; started up—got loose
from each other ; and crawled out, as well as
they could, over the horses, into the deep heavy
mud ; making wry mouths ; growling—limping
—and chafing their limbs ; all of them being
more or less beaten, bruised, or ' banged,' by the
lumber, and stuff, which, like themselves, were
inside passengers over the same outrageous, abo-
minable road."

They soon recover from this mishap, only to be
plunged into a still greater, and one which is related with equal truth and spirit. They are going
down a horrible hill at a fierce rate, in order, as
the driver says, " to keep the cattle out o' the
way o' the stage," when suddenly it is discovered
that some fire from their pipes has got among the
straw about their feet.

" The horses took fright. Away they sprang, at full speed, in the midst of the uproar, taking the heavy carriage off the ground, at every jump. Our hero leaned back into the seat, and held his breath ; for he felt as if they were tipping over, all the way—as they went—leap after leap— escaping the uptorn trees, by a sort of miracle, every time ; and shaking the driver, rudely enough to dislocate every bone of his body ; for his feet rested on a foot-board, which, in America, was attached, of course, to the rough axle-tree : Away they sprang—away—away—while the harder the poor old man shrieked, in his fear, the harder they galloped.—' Fire ! fire !' cried he —' murder ! murder !'

" ' Stop his throat, for the love o' God—whoa ! whoa !' said the driver—leaning backward into the carriage ; ' whoa ! whoa !' straining every muscle of his body, till he was red in the face ; and speaking through his teeth.—' Whoa ! whoa ! stop his throat ! whoa ! there ; whoa ! gag him ! gag him !—It's all over with us, if they get more head way !—Steady ! steady !—Jam a cloth down his throat ; or a hankycher ! Whoa ! whoa— Choke him.'

" ' There we go !—there we go !'—repeated the old man ; breaking loose from Walter, and trying to throw himself out of the carriage, over the heads of the horses.—' There we go!'

" ' Say your last prayer!—nothin' but a merigle can save us!'—cried the driver, with a voice of horrible consternation.—' There we go!—sure enough!'

" They were approaching a sharp turn—with a precipice on the left; and a steep, high bank, or wall, on the right; all the way incumbered, or broken up, with huge pine trees, or stumps, which threw their prodigious roots quite across the road.

" ' Driver! driver!'—' What say?'—' Keep to the right; will you?'—' What for?'—' Upset us, if you can—pitch us into the bank, there!' —' What for?'—' Why; there's no other hope; no other way to save a soul o' the cargo.'—The driver stood up.—' Hourra, now! hourra!' cried he; ' hourra, now—lay holt here; lay holt, every one o' you!'—throwing the reins behind him, into the carriage.—' Whoa—gently, gently, there—gent—ly—'

" ' Hang on!—hang on!—by G—d, I'll treat.' —' Hourra!'—' So will I'—' So will I!'—' Hourra, now; hourra!'—The reins gave way; the driver fell back; the carriage heeled off; the

horses tried in vain to stop—the leaders falling
back upon their fellows, when they saw the precipice, with such power, that, for a moment—a
single moment—while the strong leather cracked
with every plunge—they were all in a heap, together :—It was a moment of trial, though ; for
the carriage was tumbling over upon the horses,
while they, as if quite sensible of their danger,
were staggering about, with distended nostrils ;
and large, dilated eyes—irresolute—convulsed—
and frightfully weak—breathing, as if they had
been over-board — swimming for their lives ; a
moment of trial; but no more—a pause, only ;
for, another cry being heard—a cry of despair,
from the poor old man—up went all their heads,
together ; and off, they started, anew.

" ' Lord have mercy upon us !' cried out all the
passengers, with one voice, when they saw the
heavy manes of the horses fly up ; and heard the
crash that followed.

" ' Amen,' said Walter, very quietly ; locking
his uplifted hands ; holding his breath ; and
shutting his eyes, like a coward,—as he thought
of Edith ; and of what her insupportable anguish
would be, when they should come to hear of his
untimely fate.

" ' Amen — Amen !' — devoutly responded a steady, clear voice, at his elbow ;—' our Father, who art in heav——'

" The prayer was unfinished : the horses leaped forward, again, as if a thunderbolt had fallen among them ; two of the four broke loose from the tackling ;—one of which, went over the precipice, backward, with a scream—the other was killed upon the spot ; while the remaining pair struggled and plunged, with terrible force, under the crushing weight of the carriage.—It gave way.—' There we go !—over—over !' cried out all the passengers, with a shriek of dismay.— ' *There* we go !'———and—over they *did* go, sure enough !"

They go over on the right side, that is to say *not* over the precipice, and then, in conferring together on their escape, and the circumstances which preceded it, the following history takes place.

" ' Oh—yes !—and that air infarnal kag !' responded another.—' I do marvel what's in it ;— live eels, I guess ?—How it skipped an' bobbed about, among our toes.'

" The driver was that moment examining a small keg with great apparent solicitude. Every hoop and every stave underwent a trial with him.

" ' Gold dust, I should think,' said Walter,
who had often read of it in story books, and
poetry :—' Gold dust, I should think, by his care
of what has been spilt among the straw.'

" ' Gool' dust! fiddle-de-dee!—some sort o'
seed, more like—' quoth his neighbour ;—' some
sort o' seed, I guess ;—nothin' that's made o'
gool' is ventered here, on this road, Mister.—
I say—*you*, driver—driver ! — I say ! — what's
in that air kag ; hey ?—It aint yong'un seed ;
is it ?'

" ' Inyon seed !—pooty feller, you ! never met
with any peep seed afore, I guess ? have ye ?'

" ' Peep seed ! you cross, ill tempered, good for
nothing whelp !' cried our hero ; springing at him :
—' speak out, sir, speak ! tell him, what's in that
air keg ?'——

" ' Let go o' my throat! let go o' my throat !'

" ' Let him go,' said a young, serious man, with
a mild, but very determined air.—' Let him go,
sir—would you strangle him ?—How *can* he
speak, now ?'

" ' Never, sir—never—till he speaks out ; alive
or dead. He can do it, well enough : and if he
dooze not, before I count five ; by the God that
made me, I'll pitch him over the precipice, after

the horse ;—aye—and you too, Mr. Hale, if you interfere—we'll go, together.—What's in that air keg, sir?—one—two—three——'

" ' Powder— powder — nothin' but powder !' shrieked the ruffian, feeling himself urged, with irresistible power toward the cliff.

" ' Powder !'—echoed our boy—with a sudden leap of the heart ;—followed by a deadly sickness :—' Powder !'—his arms falling away from the collar of the wretch, as he spoke ;—' not gunpowder, surely !'

" ' Ah ;—but I rather guess it is, though !' answered the driver ; sneaking off, toward a place of safety, with a malignant shake of the head, which our hero was never able to forget, and had soon cause enough to think of.

" ' Gunpowder !—you don't say so !' faltered out one of the smokers ;—' not gun-powder !— why !' — ' Possible !' quoth his companion — gasping for breath — dropping his under jaw— and letting his lighted pipe fall out of his mouth, into the mud.——' Possible !'——' My stars !— Ugh !' "   *   *   *   *   *   *   *   *   *

" America—as every body knows, *there*—is the land of liberty and equality ; ' the land of the brave ; and the home of the FREE.' Wherefore, it would be no easy matter for a person travelling,

X

to persuade a full-blooded republican ' driver,' that
a keg of gunpowder—and a live pig—with warm-
ing pans—cod fish, broad axes, and hollow ware,
—paid for inside, were not fit company for half a
score of human beings, paid for, inside—with
lighted pipes."—Vol. II. pp. 40—68.

Nothing in its way can be more admirable than
this whole description of the boy's travel in the
" stage." It is kept up with equal force and
spirit, through forty or fifty pages more. Perhaps
we cannot do better than contrast this scene of
absolute, literal truth, with one of a somewhat
different class. It will serve to shew that our
author is not wedded to any particular style of
composition, but is equally at home in the cloudy
regions of german mysticism as on the face of
the common earth. The following, though wild,
extravagant, and incoherent, is full of eloquent
and passionate beauty. It refers to the hero's
first introduction to those scenes with which all
great cities abound.

" They led him to a sofa. They sang—they
played. His perceptions grew confused. He
thought over all the stories of wood women—
fairies—witchcraft—and sorcery. A thousand
bright flashes of early dreaming, issued from his
young heart, whenever he shut his eyes. The

room—the flowers—the furniture—the lemon tree
—the birds—the pictures—the pretty goblins—
they were like the paraphernalia of sleep, to
him. He was half prepared, for their vanishing;
half prepared, for a change, whenever he opened
his eyes, whereby they would become giants—
or dwarfs; or he would find himself at home—
after all—in his own bed. He grew sleepy—
faint. He felt as if sweet lips were saying a
sweeter incantation over him. He lay down—
he gave himself up, in spite of Harry's admoni-
tion, without one word of prayer, to the drowsy,
dangerous quiet of the place. He slept—he
dreamt; a small, soft hand was put upon his
forehead. He awoke—he started up. The pressure was gentle—affectionate; but, unpremeditated—involuntary, perhaps; yet, he started
up, quivering with preternatural fervour, through
all his frame. His head swam—his heart reeled
—his limbs were powerless. He knew not where
he was—nor what he meditated : a glowing face
—and large eyes were visible through the dim
light; a profusion of hair—and lips, that pursued his. He felt, as if he were yet sleeping; he
strove to awake. He felt as if he had gone back,
alive, to the day of mystery and fable : as if, with
all the power and prerogative; all the grandeur

—all the bravery, of a man—he had become a
little child, again ; more credulous, than ever ;
believing, as then, whatever he read—whatever
was told him ; haunting the chambers of the sea,
whenever he slept—like that of his own mother,
when he was awake.   In short—his heart was full
of woman—his head, of wine.

  " Do ye marvel that he grew dizzy ?   Do ye
wonder that he grew faint ?—or, that, he breathed, after a time, as if his heart were in travail
—every sob, a throe ?—or, that, when he awoke,
there was a strange trouble in his blood ?—or,
that, his hand fell, with convulsive eagerness
upon what he knew, by the touch, to be the hand
of a beautiful woman? or, that, he pursued it,
when it fled, with a cry of passionate longing ?
—or, that, when it should have been hastily
withdrawn from his bold—presumptuous—dis-
tracted pressure—it only trembled with fear—
until the alarm of its pulse rang, like electricity,
through every fibre of his frame ?—or, that, a
swift blindness fell upon his eyes ?—or, that, he
heard a loud singing all about him, in the air ?
—or, that, he would have spoken—but could
not—because of his youth—because of his integrity—because of his great innocence—because
of his love—in the deep, dreadful, hot, luxury

of his thought?—or, that, he drew nigh to the
tempter—and was about—boy, though he was
—to transfer the holy kiss of tried, innocent love,
to the lips of pollution?—or, that, he knew not
where he was—nor what he wanted?—or, that,
he grew blind, as it were, and sick, with passion?
—or, that, he was gathering the strange woman
—the woman of beauty—into his untroubled,
pure bosom, with all his power—in a sort of
delirium— a paroxysm — a wild, ungovernable
fervour, such as he had never felt before, in all his
life? — or; do ye marvel, that on seeing — or
dreaming that he saw—the apparition of Edith
—his own—his beloved Edith—pale and sorrow-
ful—before he had betrayed her to the woman;
before he had profaned her innocent love; sacri-
ficed her; violated her image, in his heart; or
sinned, verily, beyond forgiveness; do ye marvel
that he, the brave boy, when the spirit of Edith
went by him, thus—awoke, all at once—like a
giant; sprang away, from the enchantress, with a
sharp cry; and shook her off—the delicate, bad
creature—from his bosom—as if she were a thousand festering serpents?

"Thus did he; *thus*—and more like a timid
girl, starting from the thraldom of love, just in
time to save herself; trembling—full of sorrow

—and abhorrence—grief—gratitude—and shame: crushed with a sense of her degradation — at having been—for a moment, perhaps, under the influence of mortal treachery ; or, at having felt, for a moment, perhaps—the unholy contagion of a bad love : thus did he—more like such a girl —at such a time—than like a young, adventurous man—half crazy, with impure passion ; half desperate, with wine.   Thus did he—the noble boy.   He shook off the woman—went forth, into the middle of the floor ; smote upon it, with his foot—until the house trembled—until a thousand echoes rang through the deserted chambers, with a noise, like that of a multitude ascending the stairs—or mustering on every side of him.

" But he was alone.   Harry had left him, asleep. The woman would have stayed him ; but, when she looked into his pallid face, there was that, in it—so awful—so serious—that she went away abashed, and utterly confounded ; weeping with shame—perhaps, with sorrow—and covering her own face, with her hands.

" ' Farewell,' said he ; ' I know not who you are—nor what.   I only know that you have pursued me—till I have come to hate myself.   A little more, and I should have hated you ; all

mankind—all womankind. Nevertheless—I forgive you.'

" He departed."—Vol. II. pp. 412—417.

Where there is *any* of this kind of writing the
reader may be pretty sure of finding plenty.
What we have given above is a fair specimen of
that portion of it which the present volumes contain. In fact, they include many shorter passages, and several long scenes, belonging to the
above *class* of writing, which, together with
much extravagance, blend not a little of extraordinary beauty.

We cannot close our account of this singular
work without unequivocally expressing the very
high admiration that we feel for the powers which
it indicates : for as an *indication* alone of intellectual power can we accept it—not as a *display*.
Without being so valuable a work as some others
that might be named among the late productions
of our republican rivals, it is, without any comparison whatever, the strongest evidence of high
talent which that country has hitherto put forth.
But whether or not to regard it as a sure promise
of greater things from the same source, is more
than our total want of information respecting its
writer enables us to determine. If Brother Jonathan is the production of a new hand, and is

thrown off in that reckless and unpremeditated
manner which the construction of its plot, &c.
seems to indicate, we would at once pronounce it
to be the precursor of works of the very highest
class, and its writer as destined to occupy a permanent place in the very foremost rank of his
age's literature.   But if—as we are half-tempted
to fear, from a certain air of *practice* which prevails throughout—it is only one of many similar
incoherences which its writer has been inflicting
upon his countrymen till they will bear them no
longer, and he has now come over to try his
fortune upon *our* less fastidious and experienced
judgments, it is a very different matter.   In short,
if this is a first production in its way, and its
author is young, we should be accused of extravagance if we were to express the extent of our
hopes as to what may follow it.   But if its author has written two or three such works, we
almost despair of his ever writing a better.

BOCCACCIO AND FIAMETTA.

BOCCACCIO AND FIAMETTA;*

A TALE OF THE GREEN-WOOD-SHADE.

BY L— H—.

[As far as the writer of the following story is acquainted with
the history of the persons mentioned in it, there is no actual
foundation for its details. But he seems to have read somewhere,
within these few years, a tale in verse, the recollection of which
may have suggested it to him. And he believes, also, that Mde.
de Genlis, in her half historical romance of " Petrarque and
Laure," has imagined a passion between Boccaccio and the
daughter of king Robert of Naples.]

OF all the beautiful vales that wind about among
the beautiful hills of Italy, (like blue veins about
a young maiden's bosom), there is none so beau-

---

* Whence, or for what reason, this paper became a " Rejected"
one, I have not been able to learn. Perhaps it was, that some
editor, more sagacious than need be, fancied the writer was hoax-
ing him. And in fact, I must confess that I am a little puzzled
by the paper myself. It professes to be written by the gentleman
whose initials it bears; and I am bound to offer it as such. But

tiful as that through which the beautiful Arno lapses along beautifully, towards the blue Mediterranean.

We have passed a whole short year in this vale, reader, and can hit upon no other so compendious method of making thee feel its charms, as that of reiterating upon it the above charming epithet,—which even the language of Italy itself cannot equal, for a certain lingering and liquid softness.

Among other favours which the Arno confers upon this vale, in return for the privilege of gliding along for ever through its green loveliness, is that of writing its name upon it : Val d' Arno, or Valdarno. At a certain point of Valdarno, then, just where its scenery first begins to be most wild and cultivated, a great forest suddenly starts up almost from the river's edge, and goes frowning away towards the brow of an adjacent hill, where

though it undoubtedly includes something of the peculiar manner of that amiable writer, it seems to me to include more that is *not* in his manner, but rather in one of the manners of another writer who has also contributed an avowed portion of this volume. The truth is, I am half inclined to suspect that an innocent little deceit *has* in this instance been practised, and that the story is in fact an imitation of one of these writers' style, by the other. But which is the imitated, which is the imitator, is more than I shall pretend to determine.—*Editor*.

its rich cloud-like depths seem to hang upon the
otherwise soft and smiling elevation, like masses
of dark hair upon the forehead and cheeks of a
sweet English woman.

At the period of our story, Giovanni Boccaccio
is said to have held the office of Bard or Minstrel
at the court of Robert, King of Naples. And
whether from disgust at the hollow pageantries
of a court life, or from that morbid turn of feeling which poets and scholars are so apt to give
way to when they are forced to mix in the merely
worldly throng of which they can never form a
part,—he had for a time escaped from all inter-
course with the world of cities, and was fancying
himself content to keep no other company than
his own full thoughts, and those fine echoes and
answers to them which he seemed never to listen
for in vain among the dim glades and under the
twilight gloom of this " forest old."

That the feeling which could prompt the gay
and galliard, the lively and loving Boccaccio to
take up his abode in the solitary hut of a mountain shepherd, must have been a morbid one, who
can doubt ? Perhaps—for he was very young at
the time we speak of, and had not yet begun
to hanker after any other immortality than that
" for ever" which enters into every vow of love

which young lovers are in the habit of pronouncing—perhaps some Florentine beauty had looked inimically upon him, just when she had given him least cause to expect it,—as even Italian beauties will. Or perhaps she had smiled consentingly, just as he had begun to revel in the pleasant pains of a lover's despair; and *this* had put him out of sorts: for your youthful, and especially your poet lover, is hard to please at any moment or after any fashion but his own.

Be this as it may, certain it is that our hero had fallen out with everything in the world, but his pen-knife,—armed with which he used to betake himself every morning to the dim recesses of the old wood we have just mentioned, and carve himself out a wayward and wanton sort of comfort, by cutting verses upon the smooth bark of the great Linden trees.

There was a particular part of the wood in which a noble company of these trees flourished together, each adapting its growth to that of all the rest, in a manner which, if any but a lover had observed it, might have furnished a model from which the members of more pretending communities might have taken a lesson. It was to this spot that our sylvan malcontent chiefly directed his steps; and as practice makes perfect in all things—even in writing poetry with a pen-knife—there is no knowing how far his efforts might have gone, towards the demolition of this fine family of " green-robed senators,"—(for a Linden tree cannot live without its bark, any more than a lady's lap-dog),—but for a circumstance which we are now to relate.

Arriving about noon one day at his accustomed haunt, full, even to the tip of his pen-knife, of a sonnet he had composed as he came along, he was peering about rather impatiently for a fair sheet of bark on which to inscribe it—when lo! he observed, with a feeling of half fearful surprise, that two or three of his most passionate lucubrations had been detached from their places, and fairly carried off by some invisible, and (to him) inconceivable agency!

He dropped his extended penknife among the long grass and wild flowers that grew about the roots of the trees—retreated a pace or two from the spot where he was standing, as if to assure himself that what he had seen was not an optical trick which his over-excited fancy was playing him—and the first half dozen lines of his new sonnet went as clean out of his head as if they had been written by somebody else.

Recovered a little from his first surprise, he

began to cast about him for something like a rational explanation of this seeming mystery. But none presented itself that was at all satisfactory. He believed the wood itself to be entirely free from human inhabitants, or even visitants, except himself. . It was evident that the writing had not been defaced by any of the wild animals which he knew made their green dwellings in the forest, or even by any of the few shepherds and herdsmen who alone dwelt on its borders; for, instead of being nibbled away irregularly by the teeth of the first, or carelessly cut and scraped off by the rude clasp-knives of the second, it had been detached in the most careful manner, by making an incision above, below, and on each side of the writing, and then peeling the whole off together,—leaving the inner surface of the trunk beneath as smooth and white as the back of a new shorn sheep.

There was another circumstance, too, which perplexed our poet not a little. The particular sets of verses which had so strangely disappeared, were precisely those which he had piqued himself upon the merit of. In short, the being, whatever it might be, which had thus made so free with some of his best things, was evidently not without a very pretty taste for poetry.

This thought at any rate helped to restore our

wonderer to that state of easy self-complacency in which, notwithstanding his moody quarrel with the world, he was by no means slow to indulge himself, when his own poetry was in question ; and, instead of perplexing himself further with an affair that seemed likely to baffle all immediate inquiry, he conned over his new sonnet again, and having recovered those portions of it which his late surprise had scared away, he employed the rest of the day in carefully pen-knifing it down, at no great distance from the spot from which the others had so lately become Fugitive Pieces.   He then sauntered slowly towards his evening retreat,—wondering all the way what *could* have become of his verses, but feeling less listless and unhinged than heretofore, from the fillip which his spirits had received by the adventure of the morning.

The next day found our poet earlier than usual among his Linden trees; on reaching which, how was his not yet abated surprise of yesterday increased, at finding that his last sonnet had followed the missing stanzas, and that no trace of it was left, but the great white hiatus which indicated where it had been !

He composed no more verses that day, but passed the whole of it in puzzling his head with

Y

vain conjectures about the mystery, and in devising the means of making it out.

At last it occurred to him, (as it would two days before, to any one but a carver of love verses upon lime trees in an old solitary forest), that an act argued an agency, and that as an agent could not conveniently proceed without visible instruments, there could be no great difficulty in making out this important mystery, to any one who chose to take the pains of prying pretty closely into it.

Our poet's measures were therefore taken immediately. But before putting them into practice, there was one thing to be considered. The purloiner of his poetry (for that there *was* a purloiner seemed now more than probable to our hero, after he had given two whole days' and one night's consideration to the subject!) in the first place evidently sought concealment; and in the next place, was of too elegant and tasteful a turn of mind to be treated impertinently or cavalierly. Accordingly, our inquirer was tempted to postpone his investigation for a day or two, in order to see if chance might not give a natural turn to the disclosure ; and in the mean time he determined to try the taste of his unknown critic once more, by another copy of verses, which were such particular favourites with himself that he had not yet committed them to bark. He did so on this evening, and then went home, in lightsomer spirits than he had felt since he left Naples.

On the following morning he left his bed of leaves almost as soon as the sun looked in upon it; and after satisfying himself that he was by no means impatient to learn the fate of his last stanzas, he made his way towards the Linden trees by the most direct path he knew of; not, however, without loitering a little by the way, in order to convince himself that he was in no hurry : a piece of natural and innocent self-deceit, which, by the bye, cost him another whole day and night's increased curiosity and impatience ; to say nothing of its making him run the risk of catching his death of cold into the bargain : for at the very instant that he came, at a sudden turn of the path, upon the spot where his favourite Lindens flourished, he heard a rustling sound among the underwood at the extremity of the little glade, and caught a glimpse of a white vestment gleaming through the leaves, and saw a still whiter hand vanish away among them, and leave them quivering as if with pleasure at its touch.

To couple this unlooked-for appearance with the equally unlooked-for *dis*-appearance of his

verses, was the affair of a moment.   He flew to
those which he had carved the evening before, and
they were gone.

Here, then, was the mystery explained at once ;
but explained in a way to anything but satisfy
our hero's curiosity.   What was to be done in
this case ?   To follow the fair fugitive would be
rude, since her wish for concealment was evidently
not coquettish, but sincere.   And yet to rest
satisfied with the discovery that his verses had
not been spirited away by superhuman agency,
was quite as little to be thought of.   An alterna-
tive presented itself, which promised to satisfy his
curiosity without sacrificing his politeness; and
this he at once made up his mind to adopt.

Though he felt that courtesy forbad him to pry
into the comings and goings of this beautiful
plagiarist, (for he had already invested her with
every beauty under heaven,) he had evidently a
perfect right to pass his evenings where he
pleased ; and if he had a fancy, even, for sleeping in the open air these fine summer nights, and
making his bed on the bough of a particular tree,
there could be no doubt whatever that he was
free to indulge it.   Accordingly, he spent what
might have seemed to anybody else a more than
reasonable portion of the day in polishing into the

most graceful and sparkling perfection a stanza touching the discovery of the morning. This he carved on a convenient spot, in his best manner, and then returned to his hut, to make some little preparations for his intended *al fresco*. For, to do our poet justice, he was not one of those ill-conditioned people who neglect their personal comfort, and fancy they have taken a distaste to life and its pleasures, merely because they have happened to fall upon a particular mode of it which is naturally unsuited to them. In short, though his naturally exciteable temperament had led him to feel a sort of moody anger against certain things and people among whom he had lately been thrown, he was too young and full of health to be other than wise; his veins were filled with a stream of wholesome red blood, which ran too freely up and down them ever to permit him to be blind to the beauties of that creation which he already felt that he himself was destined hereafter to assist in beautifying.

We will not follow our hero back to his cottage dwelling, but fancy that he has been there, and provided himself with his little wallet of wine and eatables, not forgetting his graceful cloak of crimson velvet, over the collar of which his rich chesnut curls used to drop clusteringly, when, a month

ago, he justly reckoned himself among the gayest
of Neapolitan gallants.   We will fancy, too, that
he has eaten his supper of fruit with more than
usual gusto ; taken an additional cup of Cyprus,
to keep out the cold air; and comfortably established himself for the night, among the inter-
twisted branches of the very tree on the stem of
which he had carved his last piquant effusion.

He was not much disposed to sleep ; for, to say
nothing of the novel nature of his couch, with its
everquivering curtains of green leaves, his thoughts,
however pleasing, were of a nature to perplex rather than soothe—they were so entirely without
any particular point to rest on.   So that, after
puzzling himself for a long while, pleasantly enough,
but to no purpose, as to who and what the owner
of the white hand that he still saw perpetually
vanishing away among the hazel leaves could
possibly be, he was fain to yield himself up to that
voluptuous waking dream which the sights and
sounds all about him seemed expressly intended
to excite.   There was the misty and scarcely more
than twilight gloom of the old wood.   There was
the soft Italian air, sighing gently among the
leaves, and making them whisper and twitter to
each other like birds at love-making. There was the
scent of the wild-flowers, steaming up from below,

like incense from so many fairy censers. And above
all, there was the rich, deep-hearted voice of one
solitary nightingale, (made solitary, perhaps, as our
visionary fancied, by the same cause that made
him so,) bathing all things in a bright flood of
melody, as the moonlight bathes the waters.

That such a state of things as this, was not very
likely to set a poet to sleep, is pretty evident.
Whether or not it did set ours to sleep, is more
than we pretend to have been informed of. Certain it is that he saw the new day blush to life,
through the leafy lattice-work of his green bed-
room—for the first time, by the bye, since he
had taken to cultivate an intimacy with courtiers.
And he had scarcely time to reckon how dearly he
had been paying for the very equivocal pleasure of
passing for a wit and a fine gentleman, before his
whole soul and senses were absorbed in the object
which now presented itself.

In choosing out the spot that was to serve him
for a bed-room and watch-tower in one, he had of
course taken care that it should command a view
of that particular point of the wood where the
white hand had made its disappearance. And to
this point, be sure, his eyes had been constantly
directed, ever since the light had given him leave

to see it ; and directed so intensely, that, to say truth, they had no less than three times *created* the object they were in search of.   So that at last, when that object did come in reality, he was by no means sure that they were not for the fourth time making a fool of him.   But who shall describe his wondering and breathless attention, when, as he gazed, that still emerging hand was followed by a foot to match ; and then, after a moment's pause, by a face looking like a fawn's half fearfully from out the leaves, that seemed to crowd about it lovingly ; and then, after another moment's pause, the whole form emerged from among the closing bushes, and having stood for a-while as if to listen if there was any other sound than that made by the coming together of the leaves, stepped forward on tip-toe, with a hushing motion of the right hand, and with half-open listening lips, — the very picture, as our poet thought, of some fabled creature, born of the air, the twilight, and the leaves.

Alas ! it had been well for both if she had been such !   It had spared many a pang to two loving hearts, that should by rights have been lapt for ever in the Elysium of their own gentleness !   It had—but stay—we had not need anticipate.   The sad part of our story will come soon enough of itself, and will last long enough, without our letting it interfere with the happy part.

There was a hushing silence all about, as the beautiful creature kept advancing—every now and then pausing for a moment, and looking round half playfully, half timidly, towards the spot from which she had emerged, as if fearful of being seen or pursued ; while our poet kept gazing at her more and more intently, as she came nearer and nearer to the spot above which he was situated.

At last he saw the lady—(for that she *was* a lady—a very woman—he was soon pretty well convinced, if by nothing else, by the eager coursing of his own blood through its channels, and the tingling sensation which it seemed to carry with it, even to the very tips of his fingers)—he saw her approach the very tree in the branches of which he was couching, and at last come to a full stop before it.

His heart beat awfully. It fairly frightened him with its pertinacious knocking : for he had never felt anything of this kind in the presence of those court beauties among whom he had gained what little experience he possessed in matters of love. It beat—and beat—and his breath came shorter and shorter—and he grew sick with a sort of faint longing, for—he knew not what—unless it was, to drop from his concealment at the feet of that fair creature, and tell her that the poet whose poor verses she had come *all that way* to read (all the way from Florence, for anything he knew to the contrary) was there at hand, ready to pour out whole floods of them, with which the bare sight of her sweet presence had filled his soul to overflowing. .

Meanwhile, the object of this unpronounced rhapsody was standing almost immediately beneath the silent rhapsodist, quietly perusing the effusion of yesterday. She read it twice from beginning to end, before she perceived the allusion it contained to the disappearance of its fellows. But when she *did* perceive this allusion, into what a pretty blushing perplexity it cast her! She felt as if the poet himself was present in his verses, and was gazing full upon her, as *she* gazed on *them;* and she half turned round, and made a movement, as if she would have fled before that eager glance.

Our poet saw her, and was ready to drop from out his hiding place at the sight; for he thought that if once that vision melted away from before his rapt senses, (for now that the first rush of his

young blood had ceased, he began to fancy it a
vision again,) he should never either behold it
again, or be able to bear the loss of it.   But
she turned again, and stood still to re-peruse
the verses; and he was again still as a statue.

She could scarcely (as he thought) have had
time to read the first couplet again, before a
thought seemed suddenly to strike her.   She
looked away from the stem on which the verses
were graven—felt about her slender waist hurried-
ly, as if for something that was concealed in
her girdle — found it—stepped up towards the
tree eagerly—and placing one of her white hands
leaningly against the dark trunk, began to move
the dainty fingers of the other above and on each
side the spot where the verses stood.

There was no time to be lost.   She was evidently about to carry them and herself off together; and now that her furtive visits to the
wood had been noticed, she would of course never
repeat them, and he should equally of course never
see her again.

This latter thought brought back all his self-possession ; and his recollection that she was a mere
woman, and *not* a vision, came back with it.   The
next moment she started almost " like a guilty

thing," at the sound of rustling leaves and crack-
ling branches over head ; and the next, Boccaccio
was kneeling at her feet.

Fiametta (for that was the lady's name—in
thinking of her gentle nature we had almost forgotten that she *had* a name) Fiametta fairly cried
out, from a momentary mixture of terror and surprise at this somewhat startling apparition : for,
coyishness apart, it was a little startling, coming
before her as it did in the midst of a solitary wood,
when she was thinking of nothing less.   But we
must do her the injustice to say, that she did not
perform this little female feat by any means after
the most approved method in such cases made
and provided by our modern representatives of
romance heroines, either on the stage, or among
the leaves of the circulating library.   The truth is,
she did not perceive anything very frightful in the
sight of a graceful human form, bending silently
at her feet, in that attitude of adoration which
she had been taught to adopt herself, when she
sent up her innocent prayers to the unseen giver
of good ; and therefore, after the first instinctive
movement of surprise, she did not see any reason
whatever for falling into that passion of tears,
screams, and terrified supplications for pity and

orbearance, which undoubtedly ought, according
to all rule, to have been the immediate consequence
of her situation.

If indeed the object which she saw couching
before her, with its bright eyes eagerly fixed upon
hers, had been a young tiger instead of a young
man, the abovenamed mode of receiving its attentions might have been natural enough, however
unlikely to answer its intended end.   But under
the " existing circumstances," we cannot but
think that our heroine acted the more natural
part, and certainly the more agreeable one, in
merely uttering a faint hurried cry, like that of a
bird scared from its covert, and then bounding
back for a space, and shrinking up into herself, as
it were, as she gazed silently upon the silent being
before her.   At the same time, her countenance
shewed all the marks of the prettiest wonderment
in the world ; but a wonderment, withal, by no
means either angry or terrified.

But what is our poet doing and saying all this
while ?   Why, not moving a jot from his first
attitude, nor uttering a single word !   And yet
(for we must not conceal the truth) he had knelt
at ladies' feet before now, and was never accused
of any lack of words or impediment of utterance
on such occasions.

In fact, the loves and beauties of a court and
city life—even the court of the excellent King
Robert, and the city of Naples itself—however
pleasant and proper they may be, are something
different from those which are to be met with
among woods and glades : that is to say, when
any are to be met with among the latter places at
all.   And our poet was not the person to pass over
that difference, or fail to appreciate it.   In the
gentle yet blooming form of Fiametta, he beheld
what he had never seen before, even in fancy ;
though he could not help feeling,—as he gazed on
it, and it grew more blooming every moment by
the blushes that broke out all over it, — that at least
he *ought* to have seen it in fancy—else, of what
avail was his poetry to him ?   And he felt, for a
passing moment, that poetry must be but a poor
thing, if it could be put to open shame, and its
votary be surprised and dumb-foundered, before a
being who, from her air and appearance, (to say
nothing of her strangely wild and sylvan attire,)
had evidently never undergone the process of a
lover's adoration before, and scarcely seemed to
know what it could mean.

But Boccaccio was luckily a poet, as well as a
poet laureate.   It is no wonder, therefore, that all
these artificial modes of considering the matter

presently melted away, as the bright creature
before him recovered her natural and graceful
self-possession, and without shewing any very
determinate signs of departure, permitted him to
rise from his knee, and address a few phrases to
her (which, by the bye, we are bound to confess
were by no means skilfully constructed ones)
touching the situation in which the parties at that
moment found themselves.

Oh! what bright looks and what tender talk
now ensued, between this pair of gentle sylvans!
for each had been more than half enamoured of
the other before they met, and one soft interchange
of eyebeams stood them in stead of all the " give
me leave to introduces" that they ought, by rights
of wrong, to have waited for.   In a word, each
saw in the other what each had long been looking
and sighing for without knowing it; and of their
now meeting eyes was born a love that lasted—too
long.

Thus far our information has enabled us to be
tolerably precise, as to the " whereabout" of at
least one of our lovers.   And we are enabled to
add, in regard to the other, that she had been
living, ever since her birth, in a great solitary
castle at the farther extremity of the old wood;
splendidly attended, and suffered to run almost

wild about the grounds, and the adjacent forest,
like a fawn.   But she knew nothing of her birth
and condition, any more than that her father
sometimes visited her from a great way off, where
he lived.   Except him, she had seen no one that
she could remember, but the various attendants
that were about her.   These treated her as their
mistress in everything, except that they did not
seem to like her to be out of their sight for long
together;—though we have seen that she had contrived to be so two or three times, since her first
discovery of the poetical Linden trees.

All this she herself had told our (now her)
hero, before they had been together a lover's half
minute—that is to say a rather long half-hour.
Moreover, she assured him that she was " very
happy."   But it appeared evident, from something which dropped from her at the same time,
that it was the happiness of a bird that is born
in a great gilded aviary, and passes its life half
in singing for joy at what it has, and half in
pining after what it wants, without knowing what
that is.

If we piqued ourselves on being accomplished
story-tellers, we should now proceed to edify the
reader with an account of the various love scenes
which followed the above meeting.   But we do not.

If we pique ourselves on anything, it is on
having more respect for the passion of love
itself, than desire of showing our skill in developing its subtleties. So we shall here drop the
curtain of concealment upon our gentle pair of
wooers, and leave them to their own devices for
a brief space—brief in the world's calendar—
and brief even in their reckoning of it—but yet
filled to overflowing with thoughts and images
and sentiments, that spread themselves out
endlessly over their whole after life, and made
that little space seem longer than all the rest,
and yet, somehow or other, briefer than a passing
thought.

No—never shall it be said that we sought to
pry impertinently into that most holy of all precincts, the spot which is hallowed by the presence of two lovers. Let the ground all about
them, as far as their bright eyebeams can dart,
be sacred as Apollo's grove! And let their
words and looks and actions be as much their
own as their unpronounced thoughts! From
us the reader shall never hear a whisper of what
passed between these lovers, from the moment
they became such. Let it suffice that they *did*
become lovers—no " star-crossed " pair more true.
But how their great love showed itself—whether

z

in mere eye-language, or sigh-music, or whispered
words,

> " O dolci baci, o cosa altra piu cara,"

is more than we pretend to know a syllable about.
No—we leave them to each other ;—the only company lovers ever care to keep, and into which
none else should intrude, even in fancy.

Many summer days had come and gone, and
few of their suns had risen without seeing Boccaccio and Fiametta on their way to meet each
other, beneath the deep shade of the favourite
Linden trees. When one evening, as our bard
was musing within himself on a world of matters
touching the future and the past, (that is to say,
to-morrow and yesterday), but utterly unheeding
of the present, a messenger reached him from his
royal master at Naples, requiring his early presence, to assist in giving eclât to a fête of unrivalled splendour, which was soon to take place
at court, but the precise occasion of which was
enveloped in a sort of courtly mystery.

This intelligence seemed to come upon our young
dreamer " like a thief in the night." It waked
him to a remembrance that there was something
else in the world besides day-break, Linden trees,
and lovers' talk. Not that this made him un-

happy. On the contrary, it seemed to open before him a new and almost endless vista of bright hopes—every one of which seemed stamped, as it were, with the image of his Fiametta: for he felt that she *was* his, though they had not yet exchanged vows, or even recollected that there were such things as vows in the world.

They must part for a time. That was evident. But how should they meet again? And when? And under what characters? And to what end? These, and a whole string, or rather crowd of other questions, all came rushing upon his awakening fancy at once, and perplexing it for replies.

" But away with fears and misgivings!" thought our ardent hero, in the buoyancy of youthful spirits that came back with his new-born hopes. " My royal master is good and kind—and has loved, himself, they say, and therefore will not turn ungently from the tale of *my* love—and I shall gain his quick leave to return here, and seek out the father of my sweet mistress—and we will tell him how truly we love—and he shall join our hands, under a rain of tearful blessings—and we will live here, in our own forest world—and I will so people it with the bright beings of my fancy,

z 2

and so beautify it with enamoured thoughts, that the lovers of after times shall make love-pilgrimages to the spot where Fiametta and Boccaccio met, and loved, and lived, and " —— *died*, he was going to pronounce, like all the rest, triumphantly : but the thought struck a chill upon his heart, and put to flight in a moment all his fond imaginations ; for *now* that word had acquired a new and sad meaning. To die, meant, not to part from life—which had never yet entered his young imagination — but from Fiametta — which he was at this very moment called upon to do.

There was no time for pondering on the summons he had received. If he set out on the day after to-morrow, he would only just have time to reach Naples by that appointed for the solemn festival. There was nothing left, therefore, but to prepare for his departure. So he breathed forth a blithe defiance to the sad images that a word had conjured up—thought away for a moment the interval between " *now* " and that other " now " which was to make him so happy—and then laid himself down upon his simple couch, and fairly wept himself to sleep with fond yearnings after the meeting of to-morrow.

Let *that* meeting, more than all the rest, be
sacred from sight.   Let it suffice to know that
the lovers parted, as they met, happy in each
other's smiles, and still more happy in the sweet
tears that broke through them.   And Boccaccio,
without waiting for the morrow, hurried at once
on his way to Naples.   Nor did his journey lack
the accompaniment of glad songs, which told of
his happy *return* to the dark forest of Valdarno,
and the dark eyed beauty that dwelt upon its
borders.

On reaching Naples the day before the festival,
our minstrel (for he must now put on that character for a time) found that no one could give
him any information, as to the occasion of this
extraordinary gathering together of all the nobles
of the kingdom at the court of King Robert;
though many strange rumours were afloat, assign-
ing all sorts of incomprehensible reasons, and
among others, that either a new queen was to be
presented to them, or what seemed still more
unlikely, (for the king had never been married,)
an unexpected heir to the throne and kingdom.

But all this, and even all the kind and eager
greetings that met him on his return to Naples,
(for he was a great favourite with everybody,)

were "caviare" to our poet lover. He was thinking of when it would all be over, and he should be on his happy return to his now chosen retreat in the old forest of Valdarno, and within sighing distance of its sweet sylvan queen. Even the brilliant court beauties, that glided stately by him as he made his way through the well known avenues of the palace, with their earnest faces intent on the preparations for the morrow, did not stir his still thoughts a jot. They had never touched his heart ; and now that that was occupied, his senses were asleep.

Meanwhile, time passes—and the morning of the festival is come—and the great hall of the palace is thrown open—and the courtly guests are arriving in companies of two, three, four, five together, and moving along silently over the velvet floor,—their stately plumes nodding and swaying about loftily till they reach their appointed places, and then, after one deep bend forwards, settling into a quivering stillness as their wearers finally take their seats—and the banquet tables are spread out profusely, with all but the hot refections that are to be put on when the feast is about to commence—and the tall guards stand motionless at the lofty entrances—and the trimly

attired pages are passing their slim forms hither
and thither daintily—and there is a hushing and
eager stillness over the whole scene.

Let us now look away for a moment, and then
turn to the scene again, when the more lordly of
the guests are arrived, and it has put on its whole
rich completeness.   Entering upon it from the
lofty antichamber into which the great hall opens,
we will place ourselves in the great gaping door-
way itself, and look around us, just before the
signal has been given for the banquet to commence.

Right in front stretches out, strait as a line,
the rich foot-cloth of white velvet painted all over
with flowers, on which the king and his chief
nobles have just passed up the hall to their high
places.   The rest of the floor is laid all over with
crimson velvet; and for a space on each side the
centre foot-cloth, there is a vacancy, for the pages
and attendants to move about freely.   On each
side of the hall, from end to end, are placed the
tables at which are sitting, face to face, the
second rank of guests,—the princely plumes and
glittering tiaras of the dames alternating brilliantly with the dark dropping curls of the unbonneted
cavaliers, all along the double line of perspective;
while, between these at intervals, as they move

gracefully to address each other, we catch quick glances of the glittering table furniture, and see the pyramids of ornamental confectionary, and rich clusters of flowers, stand motionless. This part of the scene is finished, midway in height on each side, by the rich old tapestry which lines the walls,—the still and absorbing gloom of which contrasts quaintly with the busy brilliance which it shuts in.

Now, passing the eye upward a little on either side, it rests upon the temporary galleries which have been erected for the third rank of guests, who must be content on this solemn occasion to be spectators merely. These galleries run parallel with the side tables ; their gorgeously carved and gilded fronts projecting just even with the inner line of the table guests below. Here, in these galleries, the show of beauty is still more brilliant than below ; the plumed heads and jewelled necks being crowded more closely together, and the seats rising one behind another as they recede ; so that the bright shew reaches up to the arched and painted ceiling of the hall.

Midway between these galleries, from the centre of the arched ceiling, hang the pyramids of light that illuminate the whole scene—circle rising above circle, and diminishing as they rise, ill the upper one does but just leave space for the great twisted cord of crimson silk which supports them to pass through, and end underneath in a heavy pear-shaped tassel.

Now, passing the eye downward again towards the farther end of the hall, it falls upon the crowning richness of this bright scene. There, on a platform raised three steps above the floor, stands the royal table, bent inwards to a half circle, corresponding in size with the side ones. The surface we cannot see ; but from its hither edge depends a drapery of purple velvet, hanging down to the ground in heavy flutings—heavy with the rich embroidery-work of gold that runs round its lower edge.

On this table stand no flowers, nor fantastical ornaments ; but only a gorgeous profusion of vessels, of every shape, and for every use that can serve at a great festival ; and all golden :—not polished and glittering, as if alive with the glancing lights that they fling back from them ; but heavy, massive, dead, as if they absorbed the rich yellow rays, and grew richer and heavier as they stood.

Here and there among them, you may distinguish jewelled cups and chalices, not sparkling, but glowing, with the mingled hues of the grate-

ful emerald—the streaming topaz—the smiling
ruby—the tender sapphire—the intense amethyst
—the burning carbuncle—and the everchanging,
infinite-hued opal.

Round the furthermost side of this semicircle
of clustering gorgeousness are seated (six on each
side the centre) the twelve chief nobles of king
Robert's dominions; and in the centre of all—
distinguished from the rest only by his jewelled
crown—sits the noblest of them all, no less in
mind than in mien and bearing;—the good, the
gracious, the graceful, the kind-hearted, the high-
thoughted king himself,—more kingly in his
proud want of all pride than the merely vain ones
of the earth can conceive.

Almost immediately behind the king, (serving
at once as a dark ground to set off, and a glowing
richness to finish, that part of the scene), there
falls from ceiling to floor, and from side to side of
the hall, a drapery, full to an almost cumbersome
profuseness, of crimson velvet—all of one uni-
formly rich yet sober intensity, and only broken
at top by a second set of draperies, looped up
into heavy folds, which take a tent-like form in
the centre, and are finished at the edge by a
deep embroidered border, and a dropping fringe of
gold.

But enough of the mere externals of this
courtly scene. Its gorgeous glories are dazzling
our eyes, and keeping them too long away from
our story.

What has become of our minstrel, amidst all
this splendour?   Be sure he has not been forgotten by his princely master and friend—made
too princely by his high nature, not to feel, that
a poet's presence graces the proudest feast, and
that a poet's friendship adds a finishing lustre
to the brightest crown.

The place assigned to Boccaccio was one which,
while it made him conspicuous in the eyes of the
whole great assembly, shewed off the fine uniformity of the scene, by slightly breaking in upon it.
To every other object on which the eye seemed
called upon to rest, it might, by looking in an
opposite direction, find a corresponding object to
match. But the minstrel was seated alone, in
that otherwise vacant space left on the raised
platform by the inward sweep of the royal table.
His gracious master himself had assigned him
that place : for though he seldom remembered that
there was but one king in his dominions, he
never forgot that there was but one Boccaccio.

There our young bard sat—his head modestly
and gracefully bent forward —his eyes half-closed

and cast upon the ground—his air half-abashed,
half abstracted—and motionless as a marble
statue.

He was at that moment enjoying his glorious
poet-privilege, of living in two states of being at
once—each the best of all other states in its way.
His imagination was soaring to the high and
bright regions of poesy, in search of thoughts
and images to fulfil his appointed task ; and his
heart was walking humbly upon the green earth,
far away among the Linden trees of Valdarno.

We have not yet mentioned, that at the king's
right hand stood a vacant chair. Here, then, no
doubt, centered the high mystery of the hour.
He turned, and gave a momentary glance at that
unfilled seat—a flush of grave joy passed over his
face—and he rose up.

In an instant the busy hum was hushed, and
an utter silence seemed to fall over the whole assembly like a misty cloud.

After a moment's pause, and a look of proud
pleasure cast all around him, the king spoke.
His address was brief and simple ; not without
that terseness which it seems in the very nature
of kings to affect. He said, that he had to thank
Heaven, and he did thank it night and morning,
for a reign which had hitherto been as happy to

him as the sight of his people's happiness could make it. He said, that the love they had ever shewn for him was no less grateful to his heart, than that which he felt for them. He said, that one thing alone had seemed wanting to both, to complete the happy union between them, and make it a bond of mutual hope as well as joy. "That want," he added, after a pause, during which those who were near him might have seen a sweet thrill of delight tremble round his affectionate mouth, and his eyes fill with tears, which kept standing there while he spoke,—"That want, I fondly think, is this happy day to be supplied. For sixteen years I have been cherishing a treasure, which I have concealed from the eyes of the world with a miser's care; but only till I could try its worth, and prove it to *be* a treasure, such as it becomes a beloved king to offer to the people of his love. I *have* proved it—I *have* found it that treasure—and I now present it to the admiring eyes, and commend it to the grateful hearts, of those whom it will, I fondly hope, one day help to make as happy as I have tried to make them."

So saying, he turned half round where he stood —motioned with his hand—and as he did so, the

great velvet curtain, that hung closed behind him,
began to open in the centre, and gather itself
away into gorgeous cloud-like folds towards the
sides of the hall.   At the same moment the king
stepped back a pace or two, and led forth from
beneath it, a form whose gentleness so tempered
its beauty, that the gazers seemed to love it at
once, even in the midst of the admiring awe and
surprise that the first sight of it threw over
them.

" Behold," said Robert, " the daughter of your
king !"

In an instant a shout was uttered through the
hall, that seemed to strike against the vaulted
roof as if for escape.   It shook the flames of
the tapers till they quivered, and seemed to penetrate through all the inanimate objects till they
trembled as they stood.   But its utterers scarcely
heard it at all—so absorbed were they in the busy
thoughts and feelings of the moment.

There was *one* present who heard that shout—
and it shook her heart with an unknown fear—and
she sank silently into the seat that was near her—
and held her father's hand—and pressed it trem-
blingly.

There was *another* who heard it with a grave

joy—and it lifted him where he stood, and seemed
to place him on that highest of thrones, built up
of the hearts of his people.

There was *one* who heard it not at all. Boccaccio
had looked upon the scene with an indifference
amounting almost to impatience, till towards the
latter part of the king's address.   But when he
talked of having cherished a treasure, and " concealed it from the eyes of the world," a vague
feeling of—he scarcely knew what—seemed to
shoot through his frame, and shake it with a
strange fear ; and his attention was instantly
aroused to a pitch of intense fixedness.

As the king paused, and motioned with his
hand, a fatal presentiment seemed to seize upon
Boccaccio's breast, as it were with bodily fingers,
and almost stop his breath : but still he gazed at
the great mysterious curtain, which now began
to move.   His eye seemed to pierce like an arrow
through the opening.   At length the heavy folds
drew back, and he beheld—his gentle Fiametta !
—beheld her only for a moment — but long
enough to feel that she was *not* his, and never
could be.

The icy coldness that had been for the last few
moments gathering about his heart, seemed to

settle into its very centre—a dull, dead weight
fell upon his brain—his limbs trembled and
bent beneath him as if palsy-stricken — and
(unobserved) he sunk lifeless on the spot where
he stood.

That great shout had no more power to wake
him from his trance, than an infant's whisper.
He never thoroughly awoke from it again.   When
the momentary surprise and joy of the assembly
had subsided, and the banquet was about to commence, Boccaccio's situation was discovered, and
he was taken from the hall.

He left Naples that very night, and was heard
of no more for many months.   When he *was* heard
of, it was in his native Florence ; where his fine
spirit was flinging itself away recklessly, upon the
loose pleasures of a licentious city.

As for his sometime mistress, the splendours
of a court life disturbed and perplexed her at
first ; then dazzled and delighted her.   But when
she afterwards became the wife of the Prince of
Arragon, (to whom her father had contracted
her before he took her from her retreat), the
twilight shades and smooth stemmed Linden
trees of the old forest of Valdarno, haunted her
fancy for ever, like a dream, and cast a dim hue

of thought over her face, which did not make it less fair.

And now, do not let us leave the conclusion of our story sadder than it need be. Let us believe that if Boccaccio had not, in his early youth, met with this ill-starred "affair of the heart," he would have kept aloof from those scenes into which his sad thoughts threw him, and the world have been without that famous "Decameron" which those scenes at once impelled and qualified him to write.

☞

THE END.

LONDON:
IBOTSON AND PALMER, PRINTERS, SAVOY STREET, STRAND.

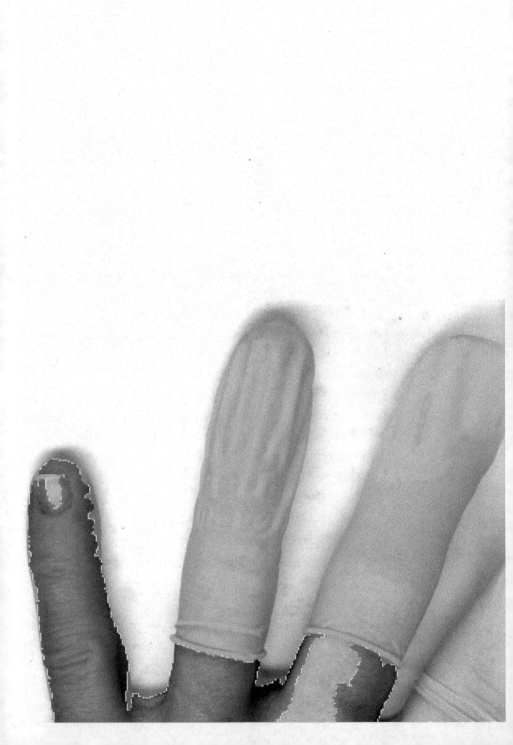

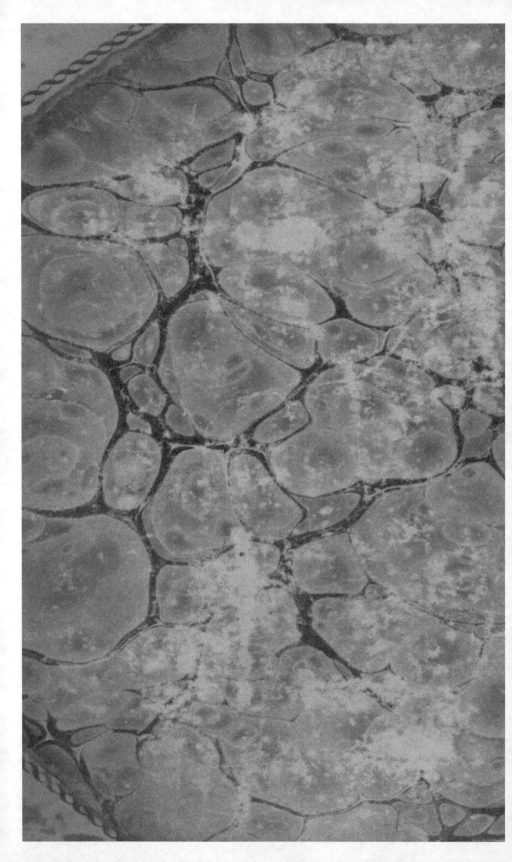

CPSIA information can be obtained
at www.ICGtesting.com
Printed in the USA
BVHW080955190819
556214BV00026B/2701/P